CRUCIFY HIM

Date D

Christ Crucified Between Two Thieves. Detail of an etching by Rembrandt, 1653.

Crucify Him: A Lawyer Looks at the Trial of Jesus
Copyright © 1990 by Dale Foreman

Zondervan Books are published by
Zondervan Publishing House
1415 Lake Drive, S.E.,
Grand Rapids, Michigan 49506

Library of Congress Cataloging in Publication Data

Foreman, Dale M.
    Crucify him : a lawyer looks at the trial of Jesus / Dale Foreman.
        p. cm.
    Includes bibliographical references.
    ISBN 0-310-51211-5
    1. Jesus Christ—Trial. I. Title
BT440.F67 1990
232.96'2—dc20   89–28924
                                                                       CIP

All Scripture quotations, unless otherwise noted, are taken from the *Holy Bible: New International Version* (North American Edition). Copyright © 1973, 1978, 1984 by the International Bible Society. Used by permission of Zondervan Bible Publishers.

The cover painting is *Christ in Bondage* by Danish artist Johann Raadsig. Used by permission of Superstock International.

Designed by Kim Koning

Printed in the United States of America

90 91 92 93 94 95 / ML / 10 9 8 7 6 5 4 3 2

CRUCIFY HIM

A Lawyer Looks at the Trial of Jesus

DALE FOREMAN, J.D.

Zondervan Books
Zondervan Publishing House
Grand Rapids, Michigan

*To my wife Gail
and our three children, Mari, Ann, and James,
who allowed me
to take time from them to write this book;
I hope their investment has been worthwhile*

Contents

Acknowledgments   9

Introduction   13

Prologue   19

PART ONE: THE ORTHODOX EVIDENCE

1. The Gospel Account   25
2. The Historical Setting   38
3. Modern Archaeology   50
4. The Reliability of the Gospels   63

PART TWO: THE NONORTHODOX EVIDENCE

5. Ancient Documents   75
6. The Apocrypha   90

PART THREE: THE TRIALS

7. The Hebrew Trial   107
8. The Roman Trial   127
9. The Punishment   137

PART FOUR: THE MODERN VERDICT

10. The Political Show Trial   *147*
11. Civil Disobedience   *160*
12. The Closing Argument   *173*

APPENDIX

Exhibit A: The Facts of the Trial   *183*
Exhibit B: Time Line of Accepted Facts   *199*
Exhibit C: Excerpts from the Acts of Pilate *204*

Notes   *212*
Bibliography   *217*

Acknowledgments

This book was written over a period of nearly ten years. I have spent hundreds of hours reading and researching the source materials. My thanks to the librarians and staff of the Widener Library of Harvard University, the New York Public Library, the Harvard Club of New York City, the British Museum in London, the Bibliotèque National in Paris, the Sterling Library of Yale Divinity School, the University of Washington, and Seattle Pacific University.

Through many drafts and revisions I have been aided by excellent research assistants: Mark Mills, J.D.; Jeff Bean, J.D.; and Eric DeJong, a third-year law student.

Friends and colleagues have read the manuscript and provided critical comments: the Reverend Dr. Thomas Duggan of the American Church in Paris; the Reverend Jonathan Sinclair Carey of Green College, Oxford; the Reverend Dr. Gleason L. Archer of Trinity Evangelical Divinity School in Deerfield, Illinois; the Reverend David Montzingo of First Congregational Church, Everett, Massachusetts; the Reverend Greg Asimakoupoulos of Crossroads Covenant Church, Concord, California; the Reverend Dr. Joseph L. Davis of Seattle Pacific University, who is a recognized scholar of the Gospel of Mark and provided many helpful insights; the Reverend Loren Jones, retired, formerly minister of First Presbyterian Church, Wenatchee, Washington; and the Reverend Al Oliver, Church of the Big Woods, Ketchum, Idaho. I am especially grateful to my father, the

Reverend Dr. C. M. Foreman, who is professor emeritus at Seattle Pacific University. He provided not only thoughtful criticisms but a lifetime of sound teaching that prepared me for evaluating the larger issues of life.

The theological interpretations in this book, unless otherwise cited, are mine. While I gained much from the wisdom of the good people listed above, any flaws in this book are strictly my responsibility.

I am indebted to those whose technical skills helped create this book. The manuscript was typed by Nancy Horejsi, Wanda White, Becky Latimer, and Bobbie Jo Carlile. The initial editing was done by Diane De Rooy. Final editing was done by Bob Hudson. In a year of reading, questioning, revising, and reorganizing, he has made this a much better book. He deserves special thanks for his wise suggestions and careful attention to detail.

Everyone is in a hurry. The persons whom I lead in worship, among whom I counsel, visit, pray, preach and teach, want shortcuts. They want me to help them fill out the forms that will get them instant credit (in Eternity). They are impatient for results. They have adopted the lifestyle of a tourist and only want the high points. But a pastor is not a tour guide. I have no interest in telling apocryphal religious stories at and around dubiously identified sacred sites. The Christian life cannot mature under such conditions and in such ways.

Eugene H. Peterson
Christ Our King
United Presbyterian Church
Bel Air, Maryland

2

Introduction

I was nearly blinded as the sunlight bounced off the water and struck the window. It was a hot, sultry day in July 1969. The train rumbled and clacked from Marseille down the coast toward the Italian frontier. I was sitting, almost asleep, looking out the window at the green-blue Mediterranean. How fortunate to be young, free, and seeing the world.

The door to my compartment slid open with a bang. A handsome dark-complected man walked in and took a seat. He wore a conservative suit, was in his middle years, and looked prosperous; yet the most interesting characteristic of this stranger was his open, inquiring face, full of good humor and subtle, cautious optimism. He greeted me in French and we chatted. He was Italian, a lawyer, a lapsed Catholic who neither believed in God nor attended church. He was a family man who thought his children were his most important responsibility and his greatest joy. In human terms, he was a good man.

As a new Christian, I was eager to share my profound happiness. After several minutes, the conversation turned to religion, and I told him of my faith in Jesus Christ. He listened intently, a twinkle in his eyes.

He was friendly but not easily convinced. My faith he called "blind," and he argued that as a rational man he saw no evidence of God. Even if God did exist, how could I be sure Jesus was his son? Why not Buddha or Mohammed? Perhaps the Messiah was an African in the jungle. To the lawyer the Bible was just Jewish mythology, while he was a man of logic and facts.

At the border the train stopped and the guards checked our passports. Since the lawyer was bound for Rome and I for Florence, we had several more miles to travel together. The compartment could seat six, but no one entered to disturb our discussion. It was as if the Holy Spirit was there, speaking to that suave Italian intellectual through a young college boy who was trying so earnestly to succeed before the train pulled into Florence.

But I'm sure that as I stepped off the train the lawyer thought of me only as a nice, pious, foolish boy from America. Although the seed of the Gospel had been sown, I was frustrated and felt like a failure. My faith was great, but I was impatient. My knowledge of the Bible and history was meager, and worse than that, I felt unable to marshal whatever knowledge I did possess. How do you convince an intellectual that Jesus is Lord?

The last words spoken by the Italian lawyer burned into my memory: "Jesus was just a prophet, a good man. But to believe he was the Son of God . . . well, that is a leap of faith I cannot take."

Since then, I have met others more open to the Gospel. Young people have seemed especially easy to approach. Several even took that "leap of faith," and their lives were changed. But still, why hadn't I been able to convince that lawyer? For years the memory of that conversation has been an incentive to me to study and learn, to improve my understanding of Jesus, and to better express my knowledge to others.

In January of 1977 one of our pastors, Loren Jones, called to ask if I would teach a Sunday school class on the trial of Jesus. He thought that as a practicing lawyer, I might have some insight into the events leading up to the crucifixion. We met and talked. It soon became obvious that he was right; I did look at the Gospel versions differently than he did. One of the first things that struck me was that the Gospels contained contradictions. More than mere variations, at times the basic facts of the story seemed to be different. Does Jesus state to Pilate that he is the Son of God or not? How many trials were there? One Hebrew and one Roman? Two of each? Or two Hebrew and one Roman? Was Jesus actually convicted? And of what crime? And why? Was the evidence convincing? Was the punishment just?

As we discussed these legal questions and the larger theological issues, my pastor suggested I spend time researching the subject and put together a seven-week series for the adults in the church. He called it: "A Lawyer Looks at the Trial of Jesus."

As I prepared, my thoughts turned to a day in early September 1972—my second day of classes at the Harvard Law School. Clark Byse, the contracts professor, called on me to state the facts of an old English case. I had spent hours the night before reading and outlining the case, yet I was confused and seemed unprepared. He attacked me savagely. "A lawyer must look at the facts and think logically. You are no longer a college student, Mr. Foreman. Discard those muddle-headed ideas about intelligence and natural aptitude. You cannot become a lawyer merely by being smart. It takes preparation and that is spelled W–O–R–K. Be prepared. Be accurate. Think clearly. Look for the facts. *Think.*"

On that second day of law school I began to think differently, though not until much later did I began to think like a lawyer. Now the process of critical analysis and careful evaluation is second nature to me. The pastor was right. Lawyers do think differently than clergymen.

I began by reading the Gospel versions of the trial. As the contradictions became apparent, it was natural for me to question the authenticity of the Gospels altogether. As a Christian I accepted the Gospels as the revealed Word of

God. As an attorney, however, I tried to go beyond my personal beliefs and look objectively at the record. This led me even deeper into the library. A serious scholar of the trial of Jesus must also study the archaeological records and read the Apocrypha, the Acts of Pilate, and the works of the ancient Jewish historian Josephus. Soon I found other books on the Jewish traditions of the trial and dozens of scholarly modern commentaries. Even then, it seemed premature to teach, for I had only scratched the surface.

The first class was small and informal. We read the Gospel versions of the trial and shared our ideas. Week by week our numbers—and our knowledge—grew. Soon we were exploring some difficult theological questions, and I felt the need to spend more time preparing on specific issues. By the end of the series our group had grown to seventy-five, and I had found in these students a newly rekindled interest in Bible study.

In 1979 I repeated the class at a neighboring church; in 1980, I agreed to update and enlarge the class at my own church. By then I had developed an outline and lesson plans. Both the senior pastor, Loren Jones, and the assistant pastor, Al Oliver, helped with the theological issues. I had a better grasp on the historical questions and the legal procedures. The laypeople in the first class responded enthusiastically. We grew to over a hundred students and had to move from the Sunday school room to the church social hall. It was a wonderful seven weeks. Our Christian growth led me to believe that an in-depth study of the trial can provide valuable lessons for all believers.

Generally, this book follows the same format as the Sunday school series. We examine the historical facts and the disputed evidence. We look at the contradictions and evaluate the Roman, Jewish, and even Moslem evidence. Although the chapters answer some theological questions, they also raise others, so a detailed bibliography is provided for those who want to read more about the trial. This book is intended to be a guide for individual or group studies, and to be of help to all who want to know more about the trial and execution of Jesus of Nazareth.

I especially hope a handsome, somewhat older lawyer in Italy will hear of this book and read about Jesus, the one called "the Christ." My message to him is that he can believe in Jesus and still be a rational, thinking man. It does not require a "great leap of faith" across an abyss of ignorance and fear. The evidence is abundant; it only takes a step.

Prologue

He hung from a rough-hewn cross. Blood ran down his legs. A crown of thorns perched at a crazy tilt on his bowed head. He had been beaten by the Roman soldiers and nailed, more than three hours before, to a hideous wooden cross. Every few seconds, as his lungs filled with blood, he gasped for breath. His body convulsed.

With great effort he arched his back to gain enough air to speak. Those nearby leaned forward to catch his last words. Whom would he curse? The hated high priest Caiaphas? Pilate, the Roman procurator? The traitor Judas? Each could expect to be cursed. It was normal for the crucified to leave this life with hate on their lips, so why should this holy man be any different?

Then he spoke.

What did he say? Those on the fringes asked the people closer up. What was it? Then they watched him cry out and die, overcome by the shock of pain and loss of blood. Everyone wanted to know—whom had he cursed, what were his last words?

But he had not cursed. Instead, he had cried out an awful and unsettling question. Quoting Psalm 22, he had said, "Eloi, Eloi, lama sabachthani?"—"My God, my God, why have you forsaken me?" (Matthew 27:46 and Mark 15:34).

The question is a troubling one for Christians. Can someone who claimed to be the Son of God die with such a pathetic question on his parched lips? Was he admitting doubts about God's plan? After the Resurrection the authors and perpetuators of the Gospels and the traveling evangelists must have been struck by the apparent inconsistency between Jesus the man of faith and Jesus the man dying with his faith shaken. Perhaps they even thought of covering up, revising, or "shredding" those words.

The Gospels of Matthew and Mark record that question as the only words spoken by Jesus from the cross. Luke and John, however, say more. According to Luke, just before the soldiers cast lots for his clothes, Jesus said, "Father, forgive them, for they do not know what they are doing" (23:34). Forgive who? The soldiers? The priests? Pilate? Herod? Judas? Peter, the disciple who denied him? The criminals beside him? The crowd? The really guilty ones? But who were the guilty ones? And what exactly had they done?

For whomever he was asking forgiveness, his request would seem to be as hopeful for Christians as his earlier question seemed unsettling. In the midst of anguish and pain beyond measure, the Man-God interceded with his Father in heaven, calling out for forgiveness. To a lawyer such a statement—called a *dying declaration*—is relatively trustworthy, because human experience has shown that people seldom die with a lie on their lips. Death is a "moment of truth," and at that moment Jesus did not curse. He blessed.

But there is a problem. Only Luke contains this question, and that Gospel, by Luke's own confession, was based on the eyewitness reports of other people—otherwise known in legal jargon as *hearsay*—evidence that is not generally admissible in a court of law. Luke was not even present. Then who heard Jesus say those wonderful words of mercy? Were they reported accurately? Did it really happen? Did Jesus really ask his Father to forgive them—whoever "they" were—while dying on the cross? Some Bible commentaries even state that certain early manuscripts of Luke's Gospel omit this important quotation altogether.

Although Luke does not mention the famous "why have you forsaken me" question, he does include two other statements. To the repentant thief, Jesus is reported to have said, "I tell you the truth, today you will be with me in paradise" (23:43); and just before dying he cried out, "Father, into your hands I commit my spirit" (Luke 23:46).

John, who was presumably standing close enough to hear Jesus speak, does not include any of the above statements in the Gospel that is attributed to him. Not one! That Gospel records many of the events surrounding the trial with a careful eye for detail, but when it comes to the crucifixion, it merely quotes Jesus as saying to his mother, "Woman, here is your son." Then he said to John, "Here is your mother" (John 19:26–27). This poignant scene seems credible: Jesus, the good son, trying to provide for his aging mother, asks the apostle to take care of her. Then after this filial piety, the Gospel reports that Jesus said, "I am thirsty," and, "It is finished" (John 19:28, 30). John was probably close enough to the cross to be addressed directly by the dying man, but the Gospel that bears his name mentions no curses, doubts, or blessings—just a tragic, painful death. Why? Did the author of that Gospel omit some statements on purpose? Did he not want to repeat what was already common knowledge? Or did he simply not hear every word?

To further complicate matters, there are many questions about the actual authorship of the Gospels. So how can we be sure they are reliable? Add to this the fact that other, nonbiblical accounts differ entirely from the Gospel record, often tracing a completely different chain of events leading up to the death of Jesus.

So what happened? Jesus of Nazareth, called by many the Christ, was crucified and died. He spoke significant words from the cross, but not even the Gospel records consistently report what he said or what he meant. He either questioned God or asked him to forgive somebody, or both—or neither. How can we, 2000 years later, hope to know what happened and what the death of Jesus means for our lives? If the Gospels are the perfect Word of God, how can they differ so much? Who actually wrote them? And what do we make of the other, less familiar versions of the story? These are the kinds of difficult questions that surround a careful study of any biblical account—and the trial of Jesus is no exception.

PART ONE

The Orthodox
Evidence

chapter 1

THE GOSPEL ACCOUNT

Before evaluating a case, a lawyer must have the facts, which involves an examination of all available documents, interviews with the witnesses, and thorough research into the applicable laws. Only then can a lawyer form an opinion about the merits of the case.

Over the past century, hundreds of authors have studied the trial of Jesus and have made available for our consideration many facts and interpretations. The bibliography at the end of this book is only a small sampling. In the next twelve chapters we will review much of this information and draw our own conclusions about these critical questions:

- What brought about the Jewish and Roman trials of Jesus?
- What actually happened?
- What happened after the trials?
- What lessons can we learn?

The best place to begin, however, is with the four Gospels themselves. In spite of the controversies, scholarship must ultimately bow to the remarkably consistent and lucid descriptions contained in these valuable documents, and, as we shall see later, many other historical sources corroborate their evidence.

In the process of collecting these facts, I hope to prove that the Gospels are authoritative and true, for the reliability of their testimony is the key to my case. Many details appear in only one, two, or three of the Gospels. A few are constant in all four. There are some inconsistencies that cast doubt on the reliability of some versions, but we will examine those later, after we have outlined the standard, generally accepted New Testament account. Here, then, is a composite version of the events surrounding the trial of Jesus.

STATEMENT OF THE FACTS

Jesus of Nazareth was the son of a carpenter named Joseph. After preaching throughout the hills of Galilee for several years and gaining many followers, he headed toward Jerusalem for the high holy days. His teachings and miracles confounded the religious authorities. The leaders of the Jews, deciding that Jesus was a threat, plotted his death.

One of the disciples, Judas Iscariot, led a band of temple police and Roman soldiers into the Garden of Gethsemane and there identified Jesus. The arrest took place at night, and in the ensuing confusion eyewitnesses were not sure whether Judas actually kissed Jesus. Jesus asked the armed men whom they sought, and when they replied, "Jesus of Nazareth," he replied, "I am he." Jesus was about to be taken away when Peter pulled out a small sword and struck at the servant of the high priest, a man named Malchus. The blow severed the ear and Jesus intervened. He healed the ear with a touch and told the disciple to put away his weapon.

Jesus asked the officers why they chose to arrest him at night rather than during the day when he taught openly in the temple. Without answering, they took him away by force. The disciples fled and Jesus was taken, bound, to Annas. They walked across the valley of Kedron and into the walled city of Jerusalem. The narrow streets were empty as they approached the house of the former high priest.

Annas held a brief hearing, informal and, as we will see, illegal. Annas questioned Jesus about his disciples and his teachings. When Jesus told him why he would not answer, an officer struck Jesus and rebuked him for his reply.

Either that night or in the morning Jesus was brought before the Great Sanhedrin, the highest religious court in Judea. It is disputed whether this group actually had the authority to execute criminals, but the court sought testimony that might condemn Jesus to death. The court attempted to solicit witnesses, but found none. False witnesses were then brought forward. At this trial the high priest, Caiaphas, asked Jesus if he was the Christ, the Son of God. Here, for the first time, Jesus answered the question directly: "Yes, it is as you say, . . . in the future you will see the Son of Man sitting at the right hand of the Mighty One and coming on the clouds of heaven."

Furious, the high priest tore his robe and cried out asking if other witnesses were necessary, for the members of the court had heard this confession. The court unanimously convicted Jesus of blasphemy and sentenced him to death. Those present began to mock Jesus; they blindfolded him and struck him, saying, "Prophesy! Who hit you?"

Jesus was then taken to Pilate, the Roman procurator. On arriving at the palace, a place known as the Antonio Fortress, Pilate came outside, for the Jews did not want to be defiled by going inside the house of a Gentile during the Passover week. Pilate asked the Jews to state what crime Jesus had committed. They replied that Jesus was a criminal, and that if he was not a criminal they would not have brought him to Pilate. Pilate responded that the Jews should try Jesus according to their laws. But a leader of the Jews quickly added that they could not put a man to death without the consent of Pilate. Pilate refused to grant them permission to impose the death penalty; he would hear the evidence and try Jesus himself. So the Jews brought forth specific charges: (1) Jesus had perverted the nation, (2) he forbade the payment of tribute to Rome, (3) he proclaimed himself a king.

Pilate asked Jesus: "Are you the king of the Jews?" In reply Jesus asked Pilate if he was asking this question for the Jews or for himself as a Roman procurator. Pilate's response was clear: "Am I a Jew?" "My kingdom is not of this world," replied Jesus. "You are a king, then?" asked Pilate. "You are right in saying I am a king. . . . Everyone on the side of truth listens to me," Jesus said. Then Pilate asked, perhaps rhetorically, "What is truth?"

Still Pilate could find no evidence of a crime, and he told this to the Jews. He discovered that Jesus came from Galilee, and since it appeared that deciding his fate could be a politically unpopular decision, he passed the problem over to Herod Antipas, the governor of Galilee. Jesus was moved again across the city of Jerusalem, to Herod's palace where he held court while in Jerusalem. He was questioned by Herod, who also wanted him to do a miracle for his pleasure, but Jesus remained silent. Herod and his guards mocked Jesus, then sent him back to Pilate.

Again Pilate told the Jews neither he nor Herod could find fault in Jesus. He wanted to release Jesus, but the crowd demanded Jesus' death. Pilate asked the people if they wanted Jesus or Barabbas released. They screamed out for the release of Barabbas. Pilate had Jesus scourged in an attempt to appease the blood-thirst of the crowd. The Roman soldiers mocked him and dressed him in a crown of thorns.

Pilate received a message from his wife, Claudia Procula, to have nothing to do with Jesus since he was a good and righteous man. Pilate questioned Jesus again, asking him where he was from, but Jesus would not answer. Pilate grew angry and asked Jesus if he understood that his life was in Pilate's hands. Jesus responded that Pilate's power was given to him from above and that those who delivered him to Pilate had committed greater sin. Pilate decided to release Jesus, but the Jews warned him that he would be condoning treason against Caesar. Pilate saw that the Jews would riot and jeopardize his political future. He wanted to satisfy the crowd but needed to somehow cleanse himself of this unjustified execution. He washed his hands publicly, released Barabbas, and delivered Jesus to the soldiers to be crucified.

SUMMATION

If I were presenting this brief in a court of law, I would tell the jury that the evidence will show that the above facts are believable, based upon accepted ancient writings, archaeological evidence, and common sense. Furthermore, as we learn more about the evidence and the criminal law of the day, we will prove that the so-called Jewish trial was illegal according to the court's own procedures and that Jesus of Nazareth was not guilty of any crime against the Roman Empire.

THE GOSPEL EVIDENCE

Of the four primary Gospel accounts, Mark, Matthew, and John are arguably based ultimately on eyewitness accounts. Although those Gospels may not be the actual written words of the disciples to whom they are attributed, I will use their names as a matter of convenience. A fuller discussion of the "authorship problem" of the Gospels appears at the beginning of chapter 4, "The Reliability of the Gospels," where I present my case for their ultimate trustworthiness.

The Gospel of Luke is by its own admission based upon

hearsay. Its author acknowledges that he has gathered his information from other sources, or as he says, "those who from the first were eyewitnesses and servants of the word" (1:2). Hearsay is defined as "an out-of-court statement or action, other than one made by the declarant while testifying at trial, offered in evidence to prove the truth of the matter asserted." The reason hearsay is so troublesome to courts and lawyers is that it is unreliable and often impossible to clarify by the normal technique of cross-examination.

Still, I intend to include Luke for two reasons. First, one of the common exceptions to the hearsay rule allows for ancient documents to be presented into evidence, as long as they are recognized as authentic. (More evidence for the reliability of ancient documents will be presented in chapter 4.) Second, since Luke's writings could be said to constitute a formal study of the events of the life of Christ, the Gospel may be considered expert testimony. Even though the author did not personally witness the events he relates, his account is consistent with the accounts of those who did. His motive is clearly to give as objective an account as possible: "I myself have carefully investigated everything from the beginning, it seemed good also to me to write an orderly account . . . that you may know the certainty of the things you have been taught" (1:3–4). If we can trust that Luke was indeed the author of his Gospel, he would certainly qualify as an expert witness. As a physician he was an educated man, experienced in dealing with people and gifted with an eye for detail.

To better organize the many important facts from these primary sources, I have arranged them into three groups in the appendix. Exhibit A.1 includes all the known facts, whether consistent or not, collected from all four Gospels. This complete composite contains 147 facts. Exhibit A.2 is smaller, being only a partial composite. It reduces Exhibit A.1 only to those facts that are explicit in one or two Gospels, but are consistent with the others; there are 100 of these facts. Exhibit A.3 is even smaller, including only the 44 facts that are both explicit and consistent among all four Gospels.

There is a fourth list, however, that is perhaps the most interesting from a legal point of view, since it includes the seven inconsistencies found among the Gospel accounts. Since inconsistencies in testimony are often the most crucial part of proving or disproving a case, I present them here. Understanding, accepting, and appreciating contradictory facts is central to a lawyer's preparation. I believe the evidence will show that these very distinctions do not discredit the Gospel versions, but serve, rather, as proof of their overall reliability.

THE INCONSISTENCIES

1. The Questioning of Jesus before the Sanhedrin

(a) In Luke, Jesus was brought before the whole council Friday morning. He was asked if he was the Christ. He responded, "If I tell you, you will not believe me, and if I asked you, you would not answer. But from now on, the Son of Man will be seated at the right hand of the mighty God." He was asked if he was the Son of God. Jesus replied, "You are right in saying I am."

(b) In Matthew, Jesus was brought before the whole council Thursday night. Caiaphas asked if he was the Christ, the Son of God. Jesus replied, "Yes, it is as you say. . . . But I say to all of you: In the future you will see the Son of Man sitting at the right hand of the Mighty One and coming on the clouds of heaven."

(c) Mark states that Jesus was brought before the whole council Thursday night. The high priest asked if he was the Christ, the Son of the Blessed One. Jesus replied, "I am. . . . And you will see the Son of Man sitting at the right hand of the Mighty One and coming on the clouds of heaven."

(d) According to John the interview took place at Annas's house, not before the Sanhedrin.

2. The Questioning of Jesus by Pilate

(a) In Matthew and Luke, Jesus responds to Pilate's question "Are you the king of the Jews?" by saying, "Yes, it is as you say." The response in Mark, as translated from the Greek σὺ λεγείς, is slightly different: "You have said so."

(b) Matthew and Mark further report that Pilate asked Jesus if he had any answer to the charges against him. Jesus remained silent.

(c) In John's account, however, the discourse between Jesus and Pilate was considerably longer, starting with Jesus' answer to Pilate's question:

> JESUS: "Is that your own idea, . . . or did others talk to you about me?"
> PILATE: "Am I a Jew? . . . It was your people and your chief priests who handed you over to me. What is it you have done?"
> JESUS: "My kingdom is not of this world . . ."
> PILATE: "You are a king then!"
> JESUS: "You are right in saying I am a king. . . . Everyone on the side of truth listens to me."
> PILATE: "What is truth?"

3. The Mocking of Jesus by the Roman Soldiers

(a) Matthew and Mark place the mocking by the Roman soldiers immediately after Pilate's sentencing of Jesus.

(b) Luke makes no reference to any mocking by Roman soldiers.

(c) John states that the mocking took place at the time of the scourging, that is, *before* Jesus is sentenced by Pilate.

4. Simon the Cyrene Carries the Cross

(a) Matthew and Mark make reference to Simon carrying the cross.

(b) Luke implies that the death march had already begun when Simon was compelled to carry the cross.

(c) John states that Jesus carried his own cross and makes no mention of anyone helping him.

5. The Repentant Criminal

(a) Matthew and Mark claim that both criminals rebuked Jesus.

(b) Luke claims that one criminal told the other not to revile Jesus, for he had done no wrong. This criminal asked Jesus to remember him when he came to power, and Jesus assured him that he would.

(c) John makes no mention of either criminal speaking to Jesus.

6. Angels at the Tomb

(a) Matthew and Luke claim there were two angels at the tomb of Jesus.

(b) Mark claims there was only one angel.

(c) Matthew, Mark, and Luke claim the angel or angels told those present at the tomb that Jesus had risen.

(d) John claims that there were two angels, but that Jesus was present in his resurrected form to tell those present that he had risen.

7. Women at the Tomb

(a) Matthew and Mark claim Mary Magdalene and Mary (the mother of James) were there to see the angel or angels.

(b) Luke claims these two Marys plus Joanna were there to see the angels.

(c) John claims only Mary Magdalene was present to see the angels and the resurrected Jesus.

DEALING WITH THE INCONSISTENCIES

It is common for critics of the Bible to attack it on the basis of such supposed inconsistencies. After extensive analysis, early pagan critics claimed to have found literally hundreds of such inconsistencies throughout the Gospels. For instance, the story of the loaves and the fishes is often cited. Jesus distributed five loaves and two fishes to 5000 people in Matthew 14:17, Mark 6:44, Luke 9:13, and John 6:9. But he also is reported to have given seven loaves and "a few fish" to 4000 people in Matthew 15:34 and Mark 8:5–7. This miracle is recounted six times in the four Gospels and is similar to a miracle performed by the prophet Elisha (2 Kings 4:42–44). In John 6:32 the miracle is related to the manna sent from heaven in Moses' time. Of course, there are explanations; these could simply be accurate accounts of distinct events.

Not only do I believe that such events are consistent on a literal level, but they are, more importantly, consistent on a spiritual level. In all the versions, the loaves and the fishes announce the arrival of the kingdom of God, declaring that the Mosaic covenant has been replaced by a new covenant and that Jesus, who in the flesh of Man is the real bread of heaven. Ultimately, the numerical inconsistencies in the loaves and the fishes are irrelevant. The lesson is the important thing in each version, and the lesson is not only consistent, but it coincides with the body of Jesus' teachings, as well as the Old Testament prophecies. Whatever the seeming inconsistencies, all the versions affirm that the event did occur.

Each Gospel may focus on slightly different facts, but not one invalidates the events themselves. In fact, while stressing different elements, all the versions point to the same general occurrences. By the same token, the integrity of the history of the trial of Jesus is intact throughout the Gospel versions.

This may not be too far off from the intent of the original

writers of the Gospels. As C. J. Ball suggests, the inconsistencies may be the result of certain cultural conditions that
we modern Americans are not familiar with.

> We have to bear in mind something that is familiar
> enough to students of Talmudic and Midrashic litera-
> ture . . . the inveterate tendency of Jewish teachers to
> convey their doctrine not in the form of abstract
> discourse, but in a mode appealing directly to the
> imagination and seeking to arouse the interest and
> sympathy of the man rather than the philosopher. . . .
>   The doctrine is everything; the mode of presenta-
> tion has no independent value. To make the story the
> first consideration, and the doctrine it was intended to
> convey an afterthought as we, with our dry Western
> literalness, are predisposed to do, is to reverse the
> Jewish order of thinking, and to do unconscious
> injustice to the authors of many edifying narratives of
> antiquity.[1]

Ball is simply saying that to the Jewish writers truth was a
matter of meaning and spirit as well as narrative representa-
tion. Though the Gospels are accurate and reliable, the
writers may emphasize different elements because their
primary goal was to convey the meanings behind the events.
  Many readers have noted the differences in the listings of
the family tree of Jesus in Matthew and Luke. Clearly, the
books contain different names. Anyone can look at them and
see gaps, a fact that has troubled Christians for 2000 years.
How could the very genealogy of Jesus be subject to error?
Eusebius, the ancient historian, quotes from an early letter
from Africanus, one of the first black Christians, to Aristides,
a Greek Christian, trying to explain these inconsistencies:

> The names of the families in Israel were reckoned
> either by nature or by law; by nature, when there was a

genuine offspring to succeed; by law, when another
man fathered a child in the name of a brother who had
died childless. For as no clear hope of being raised
from the dead had yet been given, they portrayed the
promise of the future with a mortal "raising up," in
order that the name of the deceased might be preserved for all time. These genealogies therefore com-
prise some who succeeded their actual fathers, and
some who were the children of one father but were
registered as children of another. Thus the memory of
both was preserved—of the real and nominal fathers.
Thus neither of the Gospels is in error, since they take
account of both nature and law. For the two families,
descended from Solomon and Nathan respectively,
were so interlocked by the remarriage of childless
widows and the "raising up" of offspring, that the
same persons could rightly be regarded at different
times as the children of different parents—sometimes
the reputed fathers, sometimes the real. Thus both
accounts are perfectly true, bringing the line down to
Joseph in a manner complex perhaps, but certainly
accurate.[2]

Modern scholar G. A. Williamson concludes:

The argument of Africanus must be treated with
respect. Joseph's pedigree may not matter to us, but
Christians have always been troubled, as was he, by
the apparent discrepancy between the two Gospel
accounts, which seemed to cast doubts on the reliability of one writer or both. Nor is Africanus's solution to
be ruled out. He clearly derived his information from
relatives of the Holy Family, and it must be remembered that in the Near East family trees were, and still
are, most carefully preserved; and that the "raising
up" of offspring to a childless brother must often have
occurred.[3]

So do the seven inconsistencies in the trial accounts render the Gospels unreliable? I think not. It does not matter whether Jesus was questioned on Thursday night or Friday morning, whether the soldiers mocked him before or after Pilate sentenced him, or whether Simon carried the cross part of the way up Calvary. But some details are crucial. Did Jesus claim to be the Son of God or not? Are the facts surrounding the Resurrection credible?

Unlike Africanus, I will not attempt to present a tortured analysis of every detail. It may, in fact, be impossible to rectify every discrepancy, although I believe they are probably more apparent than real. Instead, I plan to test the overall reliability of the Gospel versions against all competing and complementary accounts. For now, we must simply wait until all other evidence is in.

chapter 2
THE HISTORICAL SETTING

The trial of Jesus—perhaps the greatest turning point in history—is soon to begin. The year is about A.D. 33. The world is ruled from Rome by Tiberius Caesar. But the setting for the trial is not Rome, as one might expect, but rather, Jerusalem, a minor provincial city of the Roman Empire, a crossroads of the east, the holy city of the Jews.

The common people, the poor in spirit of whom Jesus spoke so compassionately in the Sermon on the Mount, are oppressed on one hand by the Roman soldiers and enmeshed on the other by the priests in the futile legalisms of a highly formalized religion.

THE ROMANS

The histories of Tacitus and Josephus, and the satires of Juvenal witness to the absolute power of the Roman military machine. The entire known world was controlled by force. Although wars raged on the borders, the empire was, on the surface at least, relatively stable and quiet. This Roman peace—*pax Romana*—had provided the benefits of roads,

38

improved commerce, and communication—but at an immeasurable cost in lives, suffering, and loss of freedom.

While the Romans were a religious people, they were not loyal to any one faith. Their gods were legion. By this time the Romans not only worshiped their traditional gods of Sun, Moon, Mater Matuta, Pater Tibernius, Fontas, Vesta, Lares, and Penates, but they had acquired, either by melding or outright conquest, Apollo, Mars, Neptune, Minerva, Juno, Venus, Aescupapius, Cybele, Argentarius, and 300 versions of Jupiter.

This list does not even begin to describe the extent of polytheism in Rome. The forces of nature—wind, rain, earth, fire—were deified early on, and by the time of Christ inventive worshipers had created idols and temples to Pudicitia (Chastity), Pietas (Piety), Fides (Fidelity), Concordia (Concord), Virtus (Courage), Spes (Hope), Voluptas (Pleasure), Juventas (Youth), and a host of gods were created to watch over infants and toddlers in what even then was a difficult stage of life: Junina, Statilinus, Edusa, Potnia, Paventia, Fabelinus, and Catius. The absurd extreme of this never-ending search was the creation of Tranquillitas Vacuna—the goddess of "doing nothing."

Furthermore, each time a new territory was conquered, the local gods were invited to move to Rome where a great temple would be built for them and more devoted followers recruited. By adding the favorite gods of the conquered to the already dizzying panoply of deities, Rome demoralized their subjects and ensured their continued subjugation.

Despite this religious yearning, men found little inward peace. They often did not know to whom they should pray. Some cautiously invoked the name of Janus, the god of good beginnings. Others would cry out to a long list of gods, hoping that some might have an interest in their petitions. If a supplicant was truly at a loss, he could simply pray to "the unknown god." (Readers will remember that Paul used the

Greek version of this god as a sermon topic in Athens; see Acts 17:22–34.)

Nor was prayer alone adequate. These jealous, consuming gods required sacrifices: bulls, horses, cocks, asses, sows, sparrows, doves, puppies, and even human beings. Two of Caesar's soldiers, guilty of mutiny, were executed and had their heads mounted on spears—sacrificed to appease Mars, the god of war. Sextus Pompeius ordered that some of his men and their horses be thrown into the sea during a great storm as a sacrifice to the sea god Neptune. The historian Suetonius affirms that after capturing Perugia, Augustus Caesar slaughtered 300 prisoners as an expiatory sacrifice to his predecessor, who was now considered a god himself—Julius Caesar.

In contrast to this religious yearning, the intellectual class of Romans privately mocked the myriad gods. The Roman writers Cicero and Cato openly ridiculed the hierarchy of priests, idol makers, and hangers-on who made a handsome living off the foolish god-starved Roman masses. These skeptics foresaw nothing after death but sleep. Pliny's opinion is typical of what most sophisticated Roman upper-class intellectuals believed:

> What folly it is to renew life after death. Where shall created beings find rest if you suppose that shades in hell and souls in heaven continue to have any feeling? You rob us of man's greatest good—death. Let us rather find in the tranquility which preceded our existence, the pledge of the repose which is to follow it.[1]

Although history records that Pilate offered sacrifices to the deified Tiberius Caesar (while the emperor was still alive), this was no doubt a crass, though politically wise ploy on the part of Pilate. It is likely Pilate shared the sentiments of his contemporary Seneca, who observed the religious rites of Rome only on patriotic grounds:

> A wise man will observe [these rites] as being commended by the laws, but not as being pleasing to the gods. . . . All that ignoble rabble of gods which the superstition of ages has heaped up, we shall adore in such a way as to remember that their worship belongs rather to custom than to reality.[2]

Then suddenly into this violent and wretched world came Jesus, teaching new, dimly understood truths. Not surprisingly, Pilate wondered if Jesus too was claiming to be a god; it was not an uncommon claim. Nor is it surprising that some of Pilate's questions showed a thinly veiled cynicism—that of a skeptic poking fun at a religious fanatic. For Pilate, the whole encounter was no doubt a minor footnote to his tenure as procurator of a rebellious province. On one brief afternoon of philosophical speculation, he heard this Jewish preacher share some esoteric ideas about another world. But Pilate found nothing new, no great religious teachings, no political threat. With a few hundred gods in his vocabulary, Pilate must have thought this Jesus was nothing more than a good man, an idealist, a dreamer. As a broad-minded, sophisticated Roman, how could Pilate have found any fault with that?

THE SANHEDRIN

Now we turn to the other characters in this drama—the Sanhedrin, the leaders of the Jewish nation. Most of these seventy-one men were either Pharisees or Sadducees. The Pharisees were a large group of religious conservatives who believed in prayer, angels, life after death, and a complex system of rules to demonstrate their devotion to God. They were patriotic, devoted to home, family, and study of the

Torah. To the Pharisees, who valued tradition, Jesus was a shocking new kind of rabbi, an uneducated country bumpkin who preached radical new ideas, violated the Sabbath, and surrounded himself with whores, tax collectors, and an array of poorly educated followers. As zealous and righteous men they felt a duty to stop this itinerant troublemaker.

The Sadducees were the aristocratic inheritors of the lucrative commercial temple trade. They sold doves and lambs for sacrifices—at profitable prices. They also exchanged the money of religious pilgrims and sold the half-shekel coins needed to pay the temple tax. They had a monopoly on this market and charged a four percent tax to exchange money. To Jesus they were thieves and profiteers. In their own eyes they were honest businessmen following the honorable profession of their fathers.

The Sadducees, however, did not practice the religion of their fathers with much devotion. They did not believe in angels or a coming Messiah. Some were so materialistic that they had even ceased to believe in life after death. To them, Jesus was a radical bent on destroying their temple trade and ruining their monopoly.

Jesus' conflict with both groups is pointedly illustrated by the following encounters in the temple just days before his arrest (Mark 11:15–18, 27–33):

> On reaching Jerusalem, Jesus entered the temple area and began driving out those who were buying and selling there. He overturned the tables of the money changers and the benches of those selling doves, and would not allow anyone to carry merchandise through the temple courts. And as he taught them, he said, "Is it not written: 'My house will be called a house of prayer for all nations'? But you have made it 'a den of robbers.' "
>
> The chief priests and the teachers of the law heard this and began looking for a way to kill him, for they

The Buyers and Sellers Driven Out of the Temple. A wood engraving by well-known nineteenth-century artist Gustave Doré, from his illustrated Bible of 1866. Note the three men in the background, apparently religious leaders already planning ways of getting rid of Jesus.

feared him, because the whole crowd was amazed at
his teaching. . . .

They arrived again in Jerusalem, and while Jesus
was walking in the temple courts, the chief priests, the
teachers of the law and the elders came to him. "By
what authority are you doing these things?" they
asked. "And who gave you authority to do this?"

Jesus replied, "I will ask you one question.
Answer me and I will tell you by what authority I am
doing these things. John's baptism—was it from
heaven, or from men? Tell me!"

They discussed it among themselves and said, "If
we say, 'From heaven,' he will ask, 'Then why didn't
you believe him?' But if we say, 'From men'. . . .''
(They feared the people, for everyone held that John
really was a prophet.)

So they answered Jesus, "We don't know."

Jesus said, "Neither will I tell you by what
authority I am doing these things."

So Jesus posed a problem, one the religious authorities—
Pharisees and Sadducees alike—believed the power of Rome
could resolve for them. The Sanhedrin wanted no great show,
no martyr, although it was clear they sought to make an
example of Jesus to prevent similar trouble in the future. As
the high priest Caiaphas prophesied, "It is better that one
man should die for the nation." (We will return to this theme
in chapter 10, "The Political Show Trial.")

The high priest was considered the Jewish religious leader
at that time, the closest thing the Jews had to a king since the
time of the exile centuries before. But if there was only one
high priest, why does the New Testament mention several?
For nearly a century the priesthood had grown corrupt and
politicized. The high priesthood, which for 1,500 years had
been handed down by divine command within one family, had
at the time of Christ become available for a price. Herod

began this practice, and after Rome conquered Judea, it was not uncommon to see a new high priest every year at Jerusalem.

The expression, "the council of the high priests," used by the Gospel writers to designate this section of the Sanhedrin, is therefore rigorously correct; for at the time of the trial of Jesus there were twelve former high priests. Several simple priests were also included in this chamber, but they were, in most cases, relatives of the high priests. The nepotistic and caste systems were powerful at that time, as Derembourg, a Jewish scholar, has remarked: "A few priestly, aristocratic, powerful, and vain families, who cared for neither the dignity nor the interests of the altar, quarreled with each other respecting appointments, influence, and wealth."[3]

This, then, is the historical background for the trial of Jesus. But history itself is also part of the evidence that I would like to present for your consideration.

THE EVIDENCE OF HISTORY

In discussing the historical setting, it is important to note that all the facts and events mentioned are generally acknowledged by scholars to be reliable. After the research and verification of historians of two millennia, no serious scholar doubts the facts that Jesus and Pilate lived, or that Jesus was put on trial and crucified. The trial of Jesus is one historical fact among many. (A more detailed listing of other known historical events in the centuries surrounding the trial of Jesus can be found in the appendix, Exhibit B.) The sources quoted in this chapter alone should provide ample proof that Pontius Pilate and these Jewish leaders judged an actual man named Jesus of Nazareth. The testimony of history itself demonstrates the reliability of the Gospels.

Furthermore, hundreds of millions of people have believed

that Jesus of Nazareth existed and was the Son of God. This is a prejudice that we should recognize throughout this entire analysis. The fact is, in the process of weighing the evidence, many have been convinced that it is both reasonable and intellectually respectable to put their faith in this remarkable man and to believe that he was who he claimed to be.

But many people are skeptical of the "truth" of the past. No chapter on historical setting can convince them that such events took place. How can it be proven that Pilate was a real person? Who can be sure that Jesus was a flesh-and-blood man, born in Bethlehem, raised in Nazareth, who taught the people first in the countryside and finally became a teacher in Jerusalem? These are fair questions.

Some skeptics argue that Jesus was a myth. Ancient scholars named this theory "docetism," apparently because, to them, Jesus never actually came into the world as a flesh-and-blood man but only seemed to be here. Since the eighteenth century, some authors have gone even further, asserting that the entire story was fiction—Jesus to them was just one more Hercules. What evidence is there that the Christian religion is not just a myth concocted during the Middle Ages to pacify the masses and keep the establishment in power? In response, Cambridge historian Michael Grant wrote:

> That there was a growth of legend round Jesus cannot be denied, and it arose very quickly. But there had also been a rapid growth of legend round pagan figures like Alexander the Great; and yet nobody regards him as wholly mythical and fictitious. To sum up, modern critical methods fail to support the Christ-myth theory. It has "again and again been answered and annihilated by first-rank scholars." In recent years "no serious scholar has ventured to postulate the non-historicity of Jesus"—or at any rate, very few, and they have not

succeeded in disposing of the much stronger, indeed
very abundant, evidence to the contrary.[4]

Yet if the modern skeptic wants more proof, I would ask
that our own modern calendar be introduced as evidence of
the historicity of Jesus. We tend to take our calendar for
granted. The seasons change, holidays are celebrated, our
children grow. The weeks and months go by with a regularity
that gives us confidence that planning for the future is both
wise and worthwhile. We seldom realize, however, that the
calendar itself is an evidence of God's personal presence on
earth and his power over history. Our calendar demonstrates
the mental transformation that took place in most of the
Western world as Christianity replaced paganism.

The Jewish week was a seven-day cycle based on the Old
Testament's Second Commandment to labor six days and
then keep the Sabbath holy. The seventh day became a
subject of much custom and rabbinical teaching. Since Jews
were forbidden to work on the Sabbath, it would have been a
bad omen to begin a new business venture or commence a
journey on such a special day.

Although the Romans originally observed an eight-day
week, by the third century A.D., they adopted the seven-day
system, and like the Jews they observed a Sabbath. As the
great Roman historian Tacitus explains, Saturn's day (Saturday) was a day of evil omen when all tasks were ill-starred. It
was a time to honor Saturn because "of the seven stars which
rule human affairs, Saturn has the highest sphere and the
chief power."[5] Religious Romans dedicated each day of the
week to one of these seven stars. These were in fact planets.
At that time astrologers counted only seven planets, including
the Sun as the first of the planets and followed by the Moon,
Mars, Mercury, Jupiter, Venus, and Saturn. The pagan
names given to the days of this ancient astronomical week

continue to be obvious on our modern Western calendars, even 2000 years later:

English	French	Italian	Spanish
Sunday (Sun)	dimanche	domenica	domingo
Monday (Moon)	lundi	lunedi	lunes
Tuesday (Mars)	mardi	martedi	martes
Wednesday (Mercury)	mercredi	mercoledi	miercoles
Thursday (Jupiter)	jeudi	giovedi	jueves
Friday (Venus)	vendredi	venerdi	viernes
Saturday (Saturn)	samedi	sabato	sabado

Since the Jews and Romans considered Saturday as the Sabbath, however, why do most Christians now observe it on Sunday? It is simply because the early Christians taught that Jesus was crucified on Friday and was raised from the dead on Sunday, which became known as the Lord's Day— evidence, one might insist, of the unbroken chain of belief from early times that Jesus did in fact live, die, and then rise on the first day of the week. It is documented that the early church leader Justin Martyr, who lived between approximately A.D. 100 and 165, explained this to the Roman Emperor Antonius Pius in A.D. 150:

> It is on what is called the Sun's day that all who abide
> in the town or country come together . . . and we meet
> on the Sun's day because it is the first day on which
> God formed darkness and mere matter into the world
> and Jesus Christ our Savior rose from the dead. For on
> the day before Saturn's day they crucified him, and on
> the day after Saturn's day which is the Sun's day he
> appeared to his apostles and disciples and taught
> them.[6]

This was elaborated upon by another early church father, Maximus of Turin, in the fifth century:

> The Lord's day is reverenced by us, because on it the
> Savior of the world like the rising sun, dispelling the

darkness of hell, shone with the light of resurrection,
and therefore is the day called by men of the world the
Sun's day, because Christ the sun of righteousness
illumines it.[7]

So as early as A.D. 150 the Christian church was meeting on
Sunday each week to celebrate the Eucharist and read the
Scripture. This demonstrates the direct effects of the death
and resurrection of Jesus, that enough people were convinced
of its veracity to commit themselves to honoring a new
Sabbath, a day that ran counter to both the Roman and
Jewish customs of the time.

Also, the Romans generally dated all events from the
foundation of Rome (*ante urbem conditam,* abbreviated
A.U.C.). In their scholarship they often referred to years in
relation to *Anno Urbis I* (that is, "the first year of the city").
In the sixth century the pope directed that a new calendar be
prepared that dated all events from the birth of Jesus. The
years after that date would then be dated A.D. (that is, *anno
Domini,* "year of the Lord"). He commissioned a monk
named Dionysius to do the work. This calendar, when
finished, was gradually adopted throughout Christendom and
is still in use in most of the world—more evidence of a long
chain of belief.

So something happened that changed our calendars,
redirected people's thinking, and even caused them to alter
their concepts of time. It was not the founding of Rome or
any other great city around which history pivots, but rather,
the coming into the world of a man of great importance—
Jesus of Nazareth.

chapter 3
MODERN ARCHAEOLOGY

"But what about the documents?" someone might ask. "Is there any archaeological evidence that supports the historicity of Jesus and the Gospel accounts of his trial?" We will examine these questions in this chapter.

THE DOCUMENTARY EVIDENCE

What better place to begin an archaeological analysis of the Gospels than with an agricultural lease, dated 5 B.C., for an Egyptian papyrus marsh. The property must have been extremely valuable in its time, for all documents in the bureaucratic world of the Greeks and Romans were written on papyrus. This substance, made of the processed fibers of a tall, swamp-grown reed, was highly regulated, monopolized, and expensive. The owner of this particular marsh was wealthy and careful to have the terms drafted by lawyers and written by scribes.

The document is signed by a woman named Dionysia on behalf of her son, a minor, and Hierax and Papus, the lessees. The date is within a few years of Jesus' birth a few hundred miles away in Bethlehem. It is written in Greek and sets forth the amounts due, the dates of installments, who had responsibility for expenses, and the particular currency to be used. Precise legal boundaries are set down, and the names of the previous landowners are listed.

The text, translated by E. M. Blaiklock, states in part:

> It shall not be lawful for them to pay the workmen employed more than the current wages. They shall make an extra payment of one thousand loads of papyrus with six bundles in each. They shall not use pick axes nor gather immature rushes, nor cut from boats. They shall not sell articles made from papyrus, nor sublet the area to others nor pasture their own or others' cattle in the marsh and shall remove any stray cattle at their own expense.[1]

The lessees were liable for all damage or loss caused by war, flood (the Nile flooded annually, so they must have been prepared for a certain amount of harm), governmental action, or any circumstances natural or supernatural. At the time, the Egyptians believed in many spirits, and the hard-bargaining landlord even made the lessees responsible for all losses attributable to these spirits. Things have not changed much since then. We may not think of a god of the Nile when drafting leases, but we still include an "acts of God" provision in many of our contracts.

The farmers must have thought long and hard before agreeing to sign, as it said that any failure or breach of lease "was to merit imprisonment, fine, and summary eviction" with freedom for Dionysia to foreclose on all the lessees' property until the debts were paid. This type of general guarantee was a serious risk and the tenant could not just file a Chapter 11 Bankruptcy and walk away.

Next let's examine a Jewish document found even closer to Jerusalem and within the same time frame. In 1960

Professor Y. Yadin discovered a number of priceless documents in a cave, now known as the "Cave of Letters," which included thirty-five letters belonging to a woman named Babitha. One letter reads, in part:

> In the ninth year of Emperor Traianus Hadrianus Caesar Augustus, under the consultant of Valerius Asiaticus . . . four days before the Edes of October,

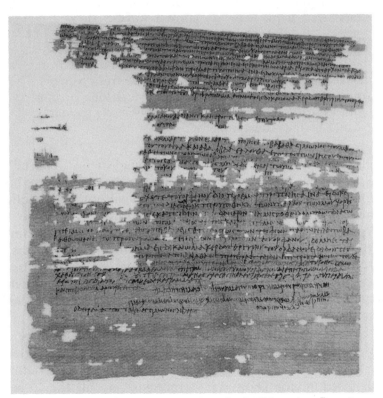

The Letter of Babitha Concerning Her Son's Education. Dated A.D. 125. Ink on papyrus, from the "Cave of Letters," discovered by Professor Y. Yadin in 1960.

and conforming to the calendar of Arabia in the twentieth year, the 24th of the month of Hyperberc-taios, locally called Thisri [October 12, A.D. 125], to Mahoza-par-Zoara, before the proper authorities.

Babitha, daughter of Simon, son of Menahem has testified against John, son of Joseph alia Egla and Abdobdat daughter of Illuta, tutors of her son the orphan Jesus, son of Jesus designated orphan by the municipal council of Petra, in the presence of these tutors, declares:

You know that you have not provided adequate support to my son the orphan. The interest you pay on his money is only one half denarius per one hundred.

I possess assets equivalent in value to the estate of my son that you hold in trust. Because of this, if you will accept my pledge as a guarantee and hypothecate my property, I will furnish interest of one and one half denarius per one hundred. The effect would allow my son to be better cared for, thanks to these peaceful times due to the administration of governor Iulius Iulianus, before whom, I, Babitha, have asked for a warrant against John, one of the tutors, for his refusal to properly discharge his duties . . .[2]

The problem faced by Babitha was that her son's education was suffering due to his tutors' low pay. The trustees of her son's estate were only paying six percent interest. Since Babitha was a woman of wealth, she proposed to guarantee payment of eighteen percent interest. The extra cash flow would give her son a better life and education.

So what do these two documents prove? A lawyer reading the lease of Dionysia or the child-support problems of Babitha would have no trouble convincing a jury that those people really existed. Scholars have studied these documents and can testify to their authenticity. The legal situations described in them are consistent with our human experience. The words, the motivations, the expressions are credible and characteristic of our species. Even though these documents are unique and quite rare, we have no difficulty believing that the papyrus field or Babitha's son existed.

The trial of Jesus, unlike the legal actions mentioned above, was an extremely well-recorded event. How much more weight and credibility that gives to the belief that Jesus was a real man. Christians, Jews, Greeks, and Romans agreed that Jesus lived as a man on the earth for about thirty years. They agreed that he taught about life and God, inspired followers, was tried, and was executed. There is much disagreement on the details of his life, teaching, and death; and his resurrection is vigorously contested. Nevertheless, the near-contemporary eyewitness accounts of his trial give us an excellent record to review, even 2000 years after the fact.

It has been the historical reliability of the Gospels themselves that has often helped to convince so many people in the truth of Jesus. The Gospels are not only historical records, however, but they are archaeological facts just as much as the lease on the papyrus field.

THE TRANSCRIPTION OF THE MANUSCRIPTS

At this point, a skeptic might raise the objection that the earliest versions of the Gospels are but copies of copies. Even though scholars confirm that the words of the Gospels were written well within the lifetimes of Jesus' contemporaries, we do not actually have the original manuscript version of Luke's Gospel, for instance, in Luke's own hand, nor do we have any infallible way of proving that the succeeding transcriptions were accurate. But in this case the law does allow precedents to be admitted into evidence, and therefore, I would like to present another piece of archaeological evidence: the Dead Sea Scrolls.

Found by a Bedouin shepherd in 1947, these are ancient

handwritten scrolls that remained hidden in a clay pot in the dry caves at Qumran for almost 2000 years. Hundreds of documents were found in these caves. Many, similar to the many papers of Babitha, concerned details of daily life: real estate deeds, contracts, a letter threatening suit, negotiations over lease terms.

The Isaiah Scroll. The oldest known complete version of any Old Testament book. Discovered in 1947 in a cave at Qumran near the Dead Sea.

The significance of these scrolls for our purposes is that the Scroll version of the book of Isaiah is identical to the next oldest extant manuscript of that book, which was transcribed centuries later. This is evidence of the reliability of the Bible as a whole and an indication that people in ancient times kept their holy books and business records as safe as possible and transcribed them with great accuracy. In a legal context, it is safe to assume that the same was true of the Gospels. Though we do not have the originals, we know from the Dead Sea Scrolls that such "holy books" were treasured and guarded, generation after generation, with much care and great attention to detail.

Another document, this time a text of the Gospels themselves, can be offered as further evidence of the same kind. It is the Sinaitic Syriac Palimpsest. A palimpsest is a manuscript in which the original writing has been washed or scraped off to receive another text. The obliteration of the original text is seldom complete, and valuable documents have frequently been recovered from such palimpsests. In 1892 a Syrian palimpsest was found on which it was possible to discern that the underlying text was the Gospels. When Cambridge professors R. L. Bensly and F. C. Burkitt examined this palimpsest, they realized that the Gospel text was not the ordinary Syriac translation, known as the Peshitta, but an older version, previously known only from a single imperfect copy in the British Museum. From this Syrian palimpsest about three-quarters of the Gospel text was recoverable. It is substantially the same version as the museum copy, although considerably older, and adds much weight to the reliability of the New Testament texts.

All this evidence suggests that the Gospels, although duplicates of other earlier manuscripts, have a high probability of being accurate. Furthermore, these duplicates—that is, our modern version of the New Testament—may be legally presented as evidence in a court of law. For although the "best evidence" rule insists that only original documents be presented, it does allow certain exceptions.

> Requirement of Original. To prove the content of a writing, recording, or photograph, the original writing, recording, or photograph is required, except as otherwise provided in these rules or by rules adopted by the Supreme Court of this state or by statute.
>
> Admissibility of Duplicates. A duplicate is admissible to the same extent as an original unless (1) a genuine question is raised as to the authenticity of the

original or (2) in the circumstances it would be unfair to admit the duplicate in lieu of the original.

Admissibility of Other Evidence of Contents. The original is not required, and other evidence of the contents of a writing, recording, or photograph is admissible if: (a) Original Lost or Destroyed. All originals are lost or have been destroyed, unless the proponent lost or destroyed them in bad faith; or (b) Original Not Obtainable. No original can be obtained by any available judicial process or procedure; or (c) Original in Possession of Opponent. At a time when an original was under the control of the party against whom offered, he was put on notice, by the pleadings or otherwise, that the contents would be a subject of proof at the hearing, and he does not produce the original at the hearing; or (d) Collateral Matters. The writing, recording, or photograph is not closely related to a controlling issue.[3]

OTHER ARCHAEOLOGICAL EVIDENCE

Graffiti

Early Christians left much evidence of their faith in Christ in many written or carved statements, known as graffiti. Archaeologists James Strange and Eric Meyers, from America and Israel respectively, have found actual Christian testimonies carved into the ancient rock beneath the Basilica of the Annunciation at Nazareth.[4] Though this Byzantine church dates from the fifth century, a small cave beneath the north aisle, and a ritual bath, or mikveh, beneath the nave predate the church.

The fact that these scholars have analyzed and verified these graffiti is important in that these men are "expert witnesses." According to modern law this type of testimony is clearly admissible, relevant, and trustworthy as we consider this case.

Testimony by Experts. If scientific, technical, or other
specialized knowledge will assist the trier of fact to
understand the evidence or to determine a fact in issue,
a witness qualified as an expert by knowledge, skill,
experience, training, or education, may testify thereto
in the form of an opinion or otherwise.[5]

Beneath the church these archaeologists found an ancient
mosaic containing the inscription: "Offering of Conon,
Deacon of Jerusalem." It is worth noting that the first word,
"offering," abbreviated in the text, is the word that is used in
Romans 15:16 and is common elsewhere in Jewish literature.
The excavators assume that this Conon is a namesake for the
famous martyr of Nazareth killed under Decius (A.D. 249–
251) in Pamphylia in Asia Minor. In court before his death,
the original Conon is reported to have said, "I am of the city
of Nazareth in Galilee, I am of the family of Christ."

Due north of the inscription of Conon is a small cave,
pointed at the back. It measures only 4.7 by 2.3 meters.
Masons plastered its walls no less than six times in antiquity.
Since the third coat of plaster included a coin of the young,
beardless Constantine, plasterings one and two must have
antedated the fourth century, though by how much it is
difficult to say. The earlier plaster includes an inscription
painted in red that seems to be a petition to "Christ Lord" to
"save thy servant Valeria." The rest is fragmented. The
excavator thinks the inscription dates to the "early Christian
centuries." The shapes of the letters lead one to conclude the
inscription is third century.

More graffiti is scratched onto the stones beneath the
church. Most are in Greek, but at least two are in Aramaic,
which is an unprecedented find. The graffiti are mostly names
and too fragmentary to read, but one of them has special
interest. It is a name that may be read either of two ways,
both of which seem to be Christian: "Christ . . . Maria" or
"Hail . . . Maria."

Other places throughout the Holy Land, many yet to be studied carefully, have thousands of bits of Christian graffiti. Scholars Benoit and Boismard have published a find of a likely third- or early fourth-century Christian cave from Bethany. In its first use it had been a cistern about 3.20 meters deep, but in the late-third or early-fourth century, a Christian community transformed this cistern into a cave-sanctuary. The builders painted the inside walls and floor with a bluish coat of plaster containing ash.[6]

The excavators found this plaster covered with no less than seventy-one graffiti in Greek (sixty-seven examples), Latin (two examples), Syriac (one example), and Syriac or Arabic (one example). In the opinion of the excavators, the earliest graffiti (no. 43) is most likely from about the fourth century. It reads: "God of the Christians, have mercy on the sinner Anamos and remit him his sins." The walls contain many Christian crosses and names in Greek, Arabic, Aramaic, and Syriac.

Pagans as well as Christians testified to the fact that Christianity had a major role in the ancient world. A Roman graffito discovered in 1856, dating from the first century, reads, "Alexamenos worships his god . . ." Above the inscription is a rough picture of a man on a cross, bearing an ass's head, a reference clearly meant to ridicule an early Christian named Alexamenos.

THE ARCHITECTURAL EVIDENCE

Some of the most direct evidence of Jesus' existence and the power of his teachings are the many ancient churches that are being studied by archaeologists. There are almost thirty places in the Holy Land that can be dated to at least the fourth century. These include the Constantinian edifices at Bethlehem (The Church of the Nativity) and Jerusalem (The Churches of the Holy Sepulchre, the Mount of Olives,

Alexamenos Worships His God. First-century pagan graffito found on a wall on the Palatine Hill.

Eleona, and the Ascension). We know these churches were of special interest to Helena, the powerful and pious mother of the first Christian Roman emperor, Constantine.

Many of these churches were established to commemorate some event in the life of Jesus. For example, at Tabgha (Heptapegon), or Seven Springs, on the northwest shore of the Sea of Galilee, stood three fourth-century churches. These early Christian meeting houses were built on the traditional sites of the feeding of the 5000 (The Church of the Multiplication of the Loaves and Fishes), of the Sermon on the Mount (The Church of the Beatitudes), and the Mensa Christi. On Mount Tabor, worshipers gathered at the church commemorating the Transfiguration. In Sychar there was a church at Jacob's well, near the place Jesus was believed to have spoken with the Samaritan woman (John 4).

Christians built churches throughout the Holy Land, often transforming existing dwellings and sometimes taking over synagogues. At Emmaus there is a house-church of Cleopas, built in A.D. 386. At Siyar el-Ghanem near Bethlehem there is a monastery and church of the fourth century, probably dedicated to the shepherds present at Jesus' birth. One kilometer away at Kanisat er-Rawat was another holy cave and chapel, complete with more Christian graffiti and also probably associated with Jesus' birth. Christians venerated spots associated with some event in the life of Christ. These locations appear to have been honored as the sites of *epiphanies,* or spirit visitations.

Although tradition may have superseded historical fact in the attributions of some of these cites, it still shows that these traditions were persistently believed. These buildings are evidence to the many people who followed the way of Jesus in the early centuries.

The oldest known Christian church has been uncovered in the ancient town of Capernaum. Some scholars even believe it to be Peter's house, originally built around 100 B.C. and later remodeled as a Christian church. Who could doubt that Jesus lived, taught, made disciples, and was the author and finisher of a faith, confronted with such a powerful exhibit? Of the archaeologists who are interpreting this fascinating ancient building, James Strange and Eric Meyers write:

> The excavators conclude that the house was founded about 100 B.C. Sometime near the end of the first century, someone plastered it three times, which may suggest conversion to a public building rather than merely the remodeling of a house (at Capernaum, stone pavements are the rule for houses). Furthermore, the absence of plain pottery correlates with a public rather than a private use for this part of the building. Finally, since pilgrims were incising graffiti of Christian character on the plastered walls of Room 1 in the second and third centuries, it is reasonable to conclude that the Christian community had converted this room into a house-church (domus-ecclesia) with the renovations of the plastered floors and walls. . . . Though one may

insist that the evidence as reported is necessary to the
excavators' conclusion (that it is indeed Peter's house
and was venerated continuously until the fourth century), it is not sufficient. As formulated, this conclusion is really a working hypothesis to be tested with
further excavation. Perhaps future investigations will
provide even more unambiguous evidence for the
student and historian. In the meantime we have,
provisionally speaking, the oldest Christian sanctuary
unearthed anywhere.[7]

All this architectural evidence is but a beginning, for
scientists discover more pieces of the puzzle every year. We
can indeed be certain that there were early Christian sanctuaries in Palestine, although only one can be dated to the first
century. Some Bible scholars expect to find other early
Christian sanctuaries in other places, perhaps even some of
the houses mentioned in the New Testament.

Although no single piece of archaeological evidence is
conclusive in itself, the accumulative weight is convincing. It
indicates that there was a man named Jesus who lived, was
tried, and was executed, after which the world was never the
same again.

chapter 4

THE RELIABILITY OF THE GOSPELS

It would be convenient for our purposes if the Gospels that bear the names of Mark, Matthew, Luke, and John were unquestionably written by those men—convenient, but not realistic. It comes as a shock to many people, especially Protestants who stress the primacy of Scripture over tradition, that the names associated with the four Gospels are, in fact, traditional appellations bearing little relation to the content of the books themselves. Not one of the Gospels specifies an author by name, though that fact alone does not discredit their reliability.

SO WHO WROTE THE GOSPELS?

The teachings and stories found in the Gospels probably existed in an oral form for many years before being written down. In those times, in fact, the spoken testimonies of those who knew Jesus were far more valuable than any written document could have been. The Gospels of Mark, Matthew, and Luke may even have sprung from a common tradition because they share much of the same material and follow the

same general outline. Due to their similarity scholars call
them "synoptic," which means they see things in the same
general way, though this is not to minimize their many
differences. John, which has much less in common with the
other three, seems to have developed from an independent
tradition, or at least from a tradition that sought to append the
life of Jesus with events that the other Gospels overlooked.

Most likely, the Gospels themselves were first written
down between A.D. 60 and A.D. 100, and those earliest
versions were probably much the same as the Gospels we
read today. Based on the arguments presented in the previous
chapter, we can be fairly certain that the transcriptions were
accurate. This fact alone gives the Gospels much credibility,
for they most certainly took their present form within the
lifetimes of the first generation of Christians. The author of
Luke, our one admittedly "hearsay Gospel," even states in
his opening paragraph that his purpose was to record the
memories of those who knew Jesus and witnessed the events
of his life.

But the question remains: Who wrote the Gospels? And if
that can't be determined, then are they based on reliable
traditions? Let's look at each Gospel in turn.

Mark. Both the evidence and the tradition suggest that this
Gospel was compiled by John Mark, a friend of both Paul and
Peter. Around A.D. 140 a Christian writer named Papias
(quoted by Eusebius) asserted that this Gospel combined
Mark's own recollections with Peter's memories of Jesus.
This assertion is well within the realm of possibility, though
many reputable scholars doubt that Mark or Peter were the
authorities behind this book.

An intriguing, though unprovable theory is that the young
man who lost his robe in Gethsemane (Mark 14:51–52) may
have been the young John Mark himself. Such oddly realistic
details give the book its credibility, regardless of authorship;
only a genuine first-person account would have bothered

recounting such an otherwise insignificant event. Whether based on the recollections of Mark or some other follower of Jesus, the important fact is that this Gospel is clearly connected with an authoritative apostolic tradition; its portrait of Christ and the incidents it relates seem fundamentally accurate and based on firsthand accounts.

Matthew. The actual authorship of Matthew has been much debated. While Papias, again our earliest source, mentions that the apostle Matthew collected the sayings of Jesus, it is not clear whether he is referring to this Gospel or another book that no longer exists. Matthew, however, contains more detailed material about the apostles themselves than any other book, though it may have borrowed other information from Mark's Gospel. This emphasis suggests that it too is closely connected with the firsthand accounts of the apostles, regardless of whether Matthew himself was the actual compiler.

Luke. Although some questions remain, few scholars doubt that Luke, a Gentile physician, wrote the Gospel attributed to him. He never names himself, but it is clear from the book of Acts, written by the same man, that the author was an intimate companion of the apostle Paul. While in the Gospel the author admits to compiling eyewitness accounts of other people, he clearly was a participant in many of the events related in Acts. Both modern scholarship and the earliest traditions point to this man being Luke, whom Paul calls the "beloved physician" in Colossians 4:14 (RSV). Luke probably had access to the written Gospel of Mark, and from other parts of the New Testament we know that the two men knew each other well. Even though Luke's account is based on hearsay, it is a careful compilation of eyewitness testimony regarding the life and teaching of Jesus.

John. More debate has raged over this Gospel than any other. For centuries its authorship was unquestioned, but most scholars now doubt that John himself wrote it. The tradition that links John's name with this Gospel came later in the second century, after the traditions of the other three Gospels had been firmly established. Furthermore, early Christians make few references to it, although they quote extensively from Mark, Matthew, and Luke. On the other side of the argument, however, no conclusive proof exists that the Gospel could not have been dictated by the disciple himself or later compiled by his followers, based on his recollections. So many details in this Gospel are unique, credible, and unmistakably personal that it would be difficult to deny its being firmly rooted in a firsthand account. John himself is at least a leading candidate as its ultimate apostolic authority. While the authorship may be debated, the book has about it that distinctive "ring of truth" that assures us that it is genuine.

One added bit of evidence for the reliability of John is that a portion of it comprises the earliest known manuscript of any New Testament book. An Egyptian document, called the Rylands Papyrus 457, contains a fragment of this Gospel, reliably dated before A.D. 150. For the manuscript to have traveled such a distance lends credibility to the book's traditional date of composition as being between A.D. 90 and A.D. 100. That could reasonably be within the lifetimes of John himself and his followers.

Ultimately, the antiquity of the Gospels and their proximity to the events themselves are the strongest arguments for their reliability, as well as the best argument against most of the apocryphal and noncanonical books. Each Gospel was in circulation in the first half of the second century. They even seemed to have circulated as a group—the Fourfold Gospel—by that time. Furthermore, it is fairly certain they were first written in the last half of the first century—within the life spans of the eyewitnesses.

Still, does their antiquity mean they are reliable? Is ancient testimony any more dependable than modern?

ANCIENT DOCUMENTS

Simon Greenleaf, a famous nineteenth-century lawyer and teacher, evaluated the Gospel accounts as if they were evidence being presented in a court of law. In a famous treatise he concluded that, yes, ancient writings in general are deemed authentic by virtue of their age. This conclusion, which seems to place a great deal of weight on age without any true critical analysis, "begs the question" by assuming that ancient writings are necessarily accurate. Still, his reasoning is not much different than contemporary laws concerning such documents. Modern courts have adopted a rule that reflects Greenleaf's assertion:

> (16) Statements in Ancient Documents. Statements in a document in existence 20 years or more whose authenticity is established. . . .

> Requirement of Authentication or Identification (a) General Provision. The requirement of authentication or identification as a condition precedent to admissibility is satisfied by evidence sufficient to support a finding that the matter in question is what its proponent claims.

> (8) Ancient Documents or Data Compilation. Evidence that a document or data compilation, in any form, (i) is in such condition as to create no suspicion concerning its authenticity, (ii) was in a place where it, if authentic, would likely be, and (iii) has been in existence 20 years or more at the time it is offered.[1]

Simply, ancient manuscripts are accepted as reliable for legal purposes, unless evidence to the contrary is produced. Anyone insisting that a document is not factual has the responsibility to present the evidence to prove the matter, otherwise known as "the burden of proof." In a modern legal setting, anyone wishing to disprove the Gospels carries the burden of proving them wrong. While it may be difficult to prove the accuracy of any particular verse in the Gospels, it is impossible, in a legal framework, to disprove the Gospels as a whole. As Greenleaf states:

> A short way back, exception was taken to the view that everything the evangelists say must be assumed correct until it is proved wrong. Should we, therefore, accept the opposite opinion, which has been locked in an agonizing struggle with it for two hundred years, that all the contents of the Gospels must be assumed fictitious until they are proven genuine? No, that also is too extreme a viewpoint and would not be applied in other fields. When, for example, one tries to build up facts from the accounts of pagan historians, judgment often has to be given not in the light of any external confirmation—which is sometimes, but by no means always, available—but on the basis of historical deductions and arguments which attain nothing better than probability. The same applies to the Gospels. Their contents need not be assumed fictitious until they are proved authentic. But they have to be subjected to the usual standards of historical persuasiveness.[2]

THE FIVE STANDARDS OF RELIABILITY

Beyond these general assertions of reliability, the "historical persuasiveness" of the Gospels can be subjected to an even stricter legal standard used to test the reliability of the witnesses. *Starkie on Evidence,* a standard text on the subject, provides an example of such a test. "The credit due to the testimony of witnesses," says Starkie, "depends upon, firstly, their honesty; secondly, their ability; thirdly, their number and consistency of their testimony; fourthly, the conformity of their testimony with experience; and fifthly, coincidence to their testimony with collateral circumstances."[3] In our case we can apply this legal test to the archaeological evidence of the Gospels.

It must be remembered that of the four Gospels Luke can be considered hearsay. I have already argued that were the author of that book himself testifying in a court of law his testimony could reasonably be considered expert testimony. But even if only his document itself were presented, I believe it would be admissible, for among the twenty-three common exceptions to the hearsay rule is one that reads: "Statements in Ancient Documents. Statements in a document in existence 20 years or more whose authenticity is established."[4] This generally reflects Greenleaf's faith in authenticated ancient documents.

All five of Starkie's standards can be applied to the Gospel evidence of the trial of Jesus, as well as to all of the Old and New Testaments in general.

Honesty

Honesty is defined as "a sincere desire to tell the truth, with no ulterior motive." From the evidence we have, there is nothing to suggest that the writers or compilers of the Gospels were of bad character or had ulterior motives in writing. Their teachings concerning a man of "perfect purity and sinless beauty" would show them, in fact, to be of exceptionally good character, and no unrighteous motive could ever have induced them to preach or die for such a righteous ideal. There is no hint of self-gain in the teachings of Christ, so it is reasonable to assume that those who wrote about him aspired to the same ideals.

Ability

Ability is "the power to observe and the memory to recall the events actually seen." This includes two parts: the powers of observation and recall, and the opportunity to witness the events in question. The Gospels were written in the time of many of Jesus' followers. The compilers or those they spoke with seemed to be quite clear in their perceptions. Their writings show a great intellectual depth and do not sound like those of fanatics or propagandists. Their recall would be accurate, for the time spent with Jesus was the most significant of their lives. The Gospels are clearly based on the memories of people who had intimate contact with Jesus and had direct knowledge of the events. Luke, as we've already discussed, wrote from dependable firsthand accounts. Thus, the ability of all these men is beyond doubt.

Consistent and of sufficient number

Consistency and sufficient number are defined as "a substantive whole that is supported, rather than weakened by, minor discrepancies and contradictions." Arguments that state a particular Gospel is untrue because it (1) does not always account for events mentioned in the other Gospels or (2) seems to contradict other Gospels, do not invalidate the facts. Omissions do not discount the substance, nor do contradictions necessarily discredit them. In fact, the seven minor inconsistencies set forth in chapter 1 bear witness to a lack of collusion among the evangelists. The books are corroborative within the realm of all four accounts, in that confirmations and new insights can be seen when the four accounts are combined. Four writers would certainly be accepted as "sufficient number."

Conformity with human experience

Conformity with human experience is defined as "acts which the great majority of mankind would accept as reasonable without specific tangible evidence." The only serious challenge to the evangelists' reliability concerns the miracles. Since miracles cannot be explained within the realm of human experience, I believe they are exempted from this challenge. A miracle is unique and can only be believed by a person who has experienced it or has the faith to believe. For legal purposes, I have deliberately focused on the trial accounts because, except for the healing of the high priest's servant's ear, they contain nothing that is outside the realm of human experience. Nor does this book focus on the greatest miracle of all—the resurrection. The reliability of the miracle accounts could be the basis for another book altogether.

Coincidence of testimony with collateral circumstances

This is sometimes called "circumstantial evidence" and is defined as "facts either not included in the subject material, or minor details therein, that in themselves are accepted as true and support the questioned document." A truthful witness is candid; he doesn't hesitate to account for details or circumstances; his testimony is of an "equal, natural and unrestrained" nature. The Gospels have this demeanor. They relate details, often trivial, and are innocent in their accounts.

When evidence is based purely on circumstance, not on direct factual assertion, it may still be credible. In fact, certain kinds of circumstantial evidence are more accurate than eyewitness identification. For example, if a train traveling west collides with an eastbound train, someone or something failed to adequately communicate the risk. The eyewitnesses may see and recall very different things, due to viewpoint, bias, or ability. But the circumstantial fact remains—in human experience it is unlikely that two engineers intentionally crash their trains together. In the case of the Gospels, the varying viewpoints do not negate the fact that the events they record actually happened.

For all these reasons, therefore, I believe it is rational to assert that the Gospels are factual and reliable. They withstand all modern legal tests of reliability, and are also supported by the collateral evidence of history, archaeology, and even the calendar itself.

PART TWO

The Nonorthodox
Evidence

chapter 5

ANCIENT DOCUMENTS

While most Christians are familiar with the Gospel accounts of the trial of Jesus, many are unaware that there is a body of literature that portrays quite a different picture. In this chapter, we will examine a wide array of ancient source material, including records of ancient Jewish, Roman, and Islamic chroniclers.

Much of this material is clearly propaganda. Although we usually think of propaganda as a modern phenomenon, an ancient variety was directed at the new Christian community and the unsaved Gentiles, the purpose of which was to tell a different version of how and why Christ died. The ancients—both Christians and their enemies—recognized that the faith "stood or fell with the sober facts of a story."[1]

Although the Gospels contain seeming inconsistencies, they are minor when compared with the discrepancies among the sources we are about to review. Keep Starkie's test of reliability in mind as you read these accounts. Do the authors seem to have ulterior motives? Are they credible? Do they seem objective and honest?

ARAMAIC TOLEDOTH JESHU

One of the best-known alternate versions of the trial comes from an ancient manuscript called the Cairo Geniza, now kept in Cambridge, England. Written in Aramaic, it is sometimes referred to as the Aramaic Toledoth Jeshu. While the text is not complete, the fragments provide nearly a hundred lines of ancient information allegedly describing the trial and execution of Jesus.

The Toledoth begins with the trial of five disciples of Christ. Present are Rabbi Joseph ben Perachiah, the Elder Marinus, Pilate, Jesus, and John the Baptist. The text states that after the disciples are executed the discussion turns to what should be done with Jesus and John. Pilate asks, "Why are [John and Jesus] worthy of death?" implying, of course, that he does not find them guilty of any crime.[2]

The rabbi suggests that the prisoners should be brought before Tiberius Caesar, who was then living at Tiberius, a small city on the west shore of the Sea of Galilee. The men adjourn to Tiberius, and there, joined by another rabbi, named Judah "the Gardener," the emperor prescribes a test, a trial by ordeal. If Christ and John can miraculously cause his daughter—a virgin—to conceive a child, they will be spared. The Jews, however, pray against such an immaculate conception, and because of their prayers the miracle fails. The prisoners are handed over to the Jews and executed. John is crucified and Jesus is both crucified and stoned. The record indicates that Jesus tries to escape, but is captured, and after his death is buried in a garden in accordance with Deuteronomy 21:23.

When the disciples claim that Christ has risen from the dead, the Toledoth states, Pilate orders the body exhumed. The corpse is dragged through the streets of Tiberius and produced for Pilate's personal inspection. Christ is then reburied. The text concludes with an ancient form of acknowledgment, listing the dates of the crucifixion and the display of the body, a curse on all apostates, and the names of the Roman and Jewish authorities who were said to have witnessed the events.[3]

Were this text not an accepted part of the Jewish heritage, it would certainly be criticized as fiercely anti-Semitic propaganda, because it was the early Christians, not the Jews, who accused the Jews of being responsible for the death of Jesus. Modern Jewish scholars tend to blame Pilate and deny any complicity of the priests. This approach can be seen in the massive *History of the Jewish People,* published by Harvard University Press in 1976. Of its 1,170 pages less than a page is devoted to Jesus, but it makes clear the author's opinion regarding who was responsible for Jesus' death:

> Among the messianic movements at the end of the Second Temple era was one that was to play a role of the greatest importance in the history of the entire human race: Christianity, whose origins are linked to the personality of Jesus of Nazareth. Like the other messianic beliefs, it developed out of the conviction that the End of Days was near; but, while the others disappeared after the death or failure of their originators, this particular movement gained in power after the crucifixion of its founder by the Roman governor Pilate.[4]

But the ancient Jewish Toledoth Jeshu does not gloss over the priests' involvement. Although it differs with the Gospels in every other way, it does corroborate the Gospels' assertion that Pilate did not find Jesus guilty and that the Jewish leaders plotted to kill Jesus in spite of Pilate's intercession. Once John and Jesus are handed over to the Jews, they are executed in the Roman style of crucifixion, admittedly the most painful and excruciating means of capital punishment known. According to these sources, the priests hated Christ so much that he was not only crucified, but later his body was stoned before burial. This detail may have been added to imply that a resurrection was impossible due to the shattered bones and the absolute destruction of the body. Even though the Toledoth Jeshu states that the Romans played an active role in the trial of Jesus, Pilate attempted to prevent Christ's death and was overruled by Tiberius.

Nevertheless, this document does not stand up to Starkie's five criteria. It is clear that the author's ulterior motive is to disprove the resurrection and discredit the nascent Christian church, and, although fragmentary, the narrative offers no evidence that the author had any special ability as a witness.

TALMUD

A somewhat different picture is presented in the Talmud, the Jewish writings that combine the oral law as it was known by the end of the second century B.C. and the rabbinic interpretations of this law, compiled between A.D. 200 and 500. One section (b. Sanh. 43a) actually reports that the trial of Jesus was a Jewish affair and that the Romans were not involved.

In a commentary on the text, Dutch scholar J. J. Huldricus states that the Talmud indicates that King Herod made the final decision. The Hakhamin, the leaders of the Sanhedrin, consult the king before arresting Jesus. All those present agree that Jesus is guilty, and they discuss the possible methods of punishment. The entire Sanhedrin is called together to deliberate and select an appropriate death sentence from the four available choices: beheading, burning, strangling, or stoning. In this version, Jesus is first strangled, and then the body is buried by the Jewish authorities.[5]

Christ's alleged guilt, as predetermined by the Sanhedrin and Herod, was a conglomeration of facts: He was born illegitimate; he followed John the Baptist, yet disobeyed him by destroying the old teachings and teaching a new Torah; and, most condemnable, his supposed miracles and his confession that he was the Son of God.

This ancient Jewish account emphasizes the role of the chief priests in obtaining the death of Jesus. The Romans were not anxious to crucify him as a seditious criminal. Pilate was only persuaded to agree after the Jews sent Jesus to his superior. Again, although this version differs from the Gospel accounts, it does support the Gospels' portrait of a Jesus whose death was sought by the high priests and who was not found guilty of sedition by the Roman procurator. (For more information on the subject of Christ as a possible revolutionary, see chapter 11.)

Although the Talmudic account confirms many aspects of the New Testament version of the trial, it obviously attempts to justify the death of Jesus on the grounds of blasphemy. It denies the miracles and Jesus' messiahship. But perhaps most telling is the fact that it has very few points in common with the other extant Jewish account found in the Toledoth Jeshu. The seven minor inconsistencies among the four Gospels pale in significance when compared to the major inconsistencies in these two accounts. Not only do the characters and locations differ, but the methods of execution are inconsistent.

What the two Jewish versions have in common is a desire to disprove the resurrection and discourage potential converts. Both have a clearly propagandistic purpose. Generally, these accounts have been called into question by modern scholars, and most experts consider neither of them to be as authoritative as the New Testament version.

JOSEPHUS

Not all the nonorthodox evidence, however, is entirely propagandistic. One of the most interesting ancient sources is the work of the late-first-century Jewish historian Josephus, whose writings are voluminous and generally acknowledged to be among the most reliable concerning ancient life. In chapter 3 of his *Antiquities of the Jews,* he discusses Jesus:

> Now there was about this time Jesus, a wise man, if it be lawful to call him a man; for he was a doer of wonderful works, a teacher of such men as receive the truth with pleasure. He drew over to him both many of the Jews and many of the Gentiles. He was [the] Christ. And when Pilate, at the suggestion of the principal men amongst us, had condemned him to the cross, those that loved him at first did not forsake him; for he appeared to them alive again the third day; as the divine prophets had foretold these and ten thousand other wonderful things concerning him. And the tribe of Christians, so named from him, are not extinct at this day.[6]

Professor S. G. F. Brandon believes that this paragraph was altered hundreds of years ago by Christians wishing to document the divinity of Christ and that it is therefore unreliable. He argues that it was slanted to appear that Josephus, although a Jew, was a converted Christian.[7] Other modern critics, including Professor G. A. Wells of Birkbeck College, London, also believe the passage has been clumsily adulterated in a pro-Christian way. Yet far more numerous are the scholars who believe the manuscripts are accurate, including Burkitt, Harnack, Barnes, and Williamson.

Later in the same book, Josephus refers to the unjust execution in A.D. 62 of James, "the brother of Jesus called the Christ." The author Ian Wilson says of this corroborating detail that the passage

> existed in a very early version of his text, together with a passage casting doubt on Jesus' messiahship. In the

third century the Christian writer Origen had expressed his astonishment that Josephus, while disbelieving that Jesus was the Messiah, should have spoken so warmly about his brother. This information from Origen is incontrovertible evidence the Josephus referred to Jesus before any Christian copyist would have had a chance to make alterations.[8]

Still, let us say, for the sake of argument, that the passage was adulterated with a pro-Christian gloss. An indication that this may be so is to be found in the opening description of Jesus as "a wise man" (a comment, however, which is atypical in Christian literature but characteristic of Josephus). Jewish scholars, such as Dr. Geza Vermes, have tried to remove all such pro-Christian elements from the passage, recovering what they believe to be at least an approximation, if incomplete, of what Josephus originally wrote:

At about this time lived Jesus. . . . He performed astonishing feats, and was a teacher of such people as are eager for novelties. He attracted many Jews and many of the Greeks. . . . Upon an indictment brought by leading members of our society, Pilate sentenced him to the cross, but those who had loved him from the very first did not cease to be attached to him . . . The brotherhood of the Christians named after him, is still in existence . . .[9]

There is excellent justification for such a restoration. The words "astonishing feats," or more literally, "paradoxical deeds," are precisely the same words used by Josephus to describe the healings of Elisha.

Every scholar would agree that Josephus was a real historian who lived shortly after the trial of Jesus. At the very least, even if the Christian gloss is removed, Josephus described Jesus as a real person, a teacher with followers, a man who performed amazing feats. This is the best possible nonorthodox evidence that Jesus lived. Josephus was a Jew. He did not believe that Jesus was the Messiah, but he was a scholar who was familiar with the Jewish expectations of a Messiah. His historical writings corroborate some New Testament details. He refers to the Jewish and Roman trials, the execution, and the reported resurrection, neither supporting nor criticizing the account. Josephus represents the best Jewish historical tradition of the late first century.

THE ROMAN HISTORIANS

From the Roman histories, there is the well-known reference to "Christus" by Tacitus:

> Consequently, to get rid of the report, Nero fastened the guilt and inflicted the most exquisite tortures on a class hated for their abominations, called Christians by the populace. Christus, from whom the name had its origin, suffered the extreme penalty during the reign of Tiberius at the hands of one of our procurators, Pontius Pilate, and a most mischievous superstition, thus checked for the moment, again broke out not only in Judaea, the first source of the evil, but even in Rome, where all things hideous and shameful from every part of the world find their center and become popular. Accordingly, an arrest was first made of all who pleaded guilty; then, upon their information, an immense multitude was convicted, not so much of the crime of firing the city, as of hatred against mankind. Mockery of every sort was added to their deaths. Covered with the skins of beasts, they were torn by dogs and perished, or were nailed to crosses, or were doomed to the flames and burnt, to serve as a nightly illumination, when daylight had expired.[10]

Seutonius, another Roman historian, refers to some Jews of Rome who during the reign of Claudius rebelled at the instigation of "Chrestus," although it cannot be conclusively established that this is in fact Jesus.

Finally, Pliny the Younger, as governor of Bithynia, wrote to the Emperor Trajan in A.D. 112, reporting that the Christians were apparently a harmless group of people who met at daybreak and sang hymns to the Messiah. Pliny commented, "I could discover nothing more than a depraved and excessive superstition."[11]

At the very least, these accounts demonstrate that Jesus lived and influenced many people, even if these writings do not refer specifically to his trial.

THE APOLOGY OF ARISTIDES

In 1889 J. Rendel Harris, a young Cambridge scholar, found in the monastery of St. Catherine a Syriac translation of a book called the Apology of Aristides. It was a defense of Christianity that is mentioned by Eusebius, who says that it was addressed to the Emperor Hadrian in A.D. 125. As an eloquent eulogy of Christianity, it exposes the failures of the barbarians, Greeks, and Jews to realize the true nature of God, and draws a picture of the Christian community. It contains no quotations from the Gospels, but reference is made to the "writings of the Christians," and the main points of the Christian creed are summarized. In 1922 the British Museum acquired two leaves of a papyrus from the fourth century, one of which contained part of the Apology of Aristides in Greek. While experts believe the Syriac version was written first and the Greek was a later abridgment, both are from the earliest post-apostolic period.

THE DIATESSARON OF TATIAN

Another manuscript connected with the Syrian church has come to light within the last hundred years. Eusebius wrote that a man named Tatian composed a harmony of the four Gospels, called the Diatessaron, a musical term denoting a harmony of four elements. It circulated widely in the Syrian church. Tatian, a Syrian by birth, became a disciple of Justin Martyr at Rome, where he wrote an Apology for Christianity. But after Justin's death in A.D. 165 Tatian's ascetic opinions were condemned as heretical, and he returned to his native land, where he died about A.D. 180. The Diatessaron disappeared for centuries. In 1880 an American scholar, Dr. Ezra Abbot, discovered that in 1836 the Armenian fathers of the Mechitarist monastery in Venice had published an Armenian version of a commentary on the Diatessaron by St. Ephraem of Syria, who died in A.D. 373. The discovery stimulated further scholarship and two copies of an Arabic version of the Diatessaron itself came to light, one in Rome and one in Cairo. In the sixth century Bishop Victor of Capua found a harmony of the Gospels in Latin. He guessed that it was the work referred to by Eusebius, and he had it transcribed between A.D. 541–46. That copy is now in the Abbey of Fulda.

So what do these documents mean? As Professor Joseph L. Davis has commented:

> Sacred tradition was almost surely far more tenacious in a largely preliterate society than the modern world can well imagine. Thus, both oral tradition and eyewitness testimony transmitted by followers have much more to be said for their reliability than would be thought in our modern world where so much more dependability seems to be guaranteed by a written record. . . .

Tatian decided that one Gospel would be better than four. He homogenized the Gospels and produced the Diatessaron. That result dominated Syrian Christianity for a lengthy period. As I see it, the Christian community is fortunate that the four separate Gospels rather than Tatian won that war.

So we are stuck, thank God, with the witness of four diverse Gospels whose witness to truth makes more believable rather than less the Gospel of Jesus Christ.[12]

THE KORAN

Finally, let's examine an unlikely bit of evidence: the Moslem holy book, the Koran. A lawyer would call this using an adverse, or hostile witness, but the Koran, the words of the Muhammad, speak repeatedly of Jesus.

Muhammad was an illiterate shepherd who, at age twenty-four, married a wealthy widow, Khadija, who was then nearly forty. He helped her manage her assets and was regarded as a shrewd trader. At times he would go into the hills and meditate at a cave on Mount Hira near Mecca. There on the Night of Qadr (the night of power, or glory) in the year A.D. 610 he had a vision of the angel Gabriel who commanded him to "Recite!" Over a period of years Muhammad wrote down many revelations, claiming to be God's messenger on earth. His writings became the Koran, and his teachings centered on the five pillars of faith, the first of which is the profession of faith, the *shahada:* "There is no god but Allah and Muhammad is His prophet."

Several scholars believe "Muhammad never intended to make Islam a new religion." J. A. Montgomery and Abraham Katsch, one a Christian, the other a Jew, assert that Muhammad saw no difference between Christianity and Judaism and was nearly converted to Judaism. He expected both groups to receive him as the "Seal of the Prophets."

When they rejected him, he turned his back on them and even changed his holy city from Jerusalem to Mecca.[13]

To a follower of Islam, there is only one god—Allah. The jealous god of the Moslems is a single undivided being. The Koran says: "Allah is one, the Eternal God. He begot none, nor was he begotten. None is equal to him" (Sura 112). While Jesus was a good man, according to Muhammad, his followers who taught the Trinity committed a horrible blasphemy: "Those who say, 'The Lord of Mercy has begotten a Son,' preach a monstrous falsehood, at which the very heavens might crack, the earth break asunder and the mountains crumble to dust. That they should ascribe a son to the Merciful, when it does not become Him to beget one!" (Koran 19:88).

At first Muhammad had attempted to build on the Jewish and Christian religious foundations. He wanted respect and a puritanical devotion. He wanted to be considered equal to Moses or Jesus, specially appointed by Allah to guide the Arabs toward monotheistic truth. But both Christians and Jews rejected him and ridiculed his interpretation of their Scriptures. Both taught that he was a false prophet.

Muhammad then responded to his critics, "They have said: 'None but Jews and Christians shall enter into paradise.' Such are their wishful fancies. Say: 'Let us have proof, if what you say is true.' No. He that surrenders himself to Allah and does what is right shall have his reward with his Lord" (Koran ii, 105–6).

Muhammad considered Jesus a great prophet, however. As described in the Koran, Jesus was called *al-masih* (the Messiah), a word borrowed from Syriac or Ethiopic, which in Arabic could also mean "the anointed." His mother, Mary, the sister of Aaron and hence of Moses, had been warned by angels that she would conceive without having known a man and bear a remarkable son:

> A Word from him Allah and his name shall be the
> Messiah, Isa, son of Maryam. He shall be noble in this
> world and in the next, and shall be of those close [to
> the throne]. He shall speak to men from his cradle. . . .
> [Allah] will instruct him in the Book and in Wisdom,
> the Torah and the Injil [Gospel]. (Koran iii, 40–43)

In one controversial verse of the Koran, Sura II verse 254,
Muhammad even seems to rank Jesus as the preferred or
foremost prophet:

> The apostles have we preferred one of them above
> another. Of them is one to whom God spake; and we
> have raised some of them degrees; and we have given
> Jesus the son of Mary manifest signs, and strengthened
> him by the Holy Spirit. And, did God please, those
> who came after them would not have fought after there
> came to them manifest signs. But they did disagree,
> and of them are some who believe, and of them some
> who misbelieve, but, did God please, they would not
> have fought, for God does what He will.

Muhammad taught that this miracle came to pass because
Allah had sent some of his Spirit into Mary. This was a
prophet sent by Allah to the Israelites. Jesus had come into
the world and worked many miracles. Even as a child he
made birds out of clay and breathed life into them. He cured
the dumb and the lepers and resurrected the dead. The Jews
boasted of having killed him but this was not true. They had
been victims of a mirage, a ruse on the part of Allah. They
believed they had crucified him, but in fact "Allah raised him
to himself" (Koran iv, 156). He was with his mother "on a
hill peaceful and well-watered" (Koran xxiii, 52).

Muhammad must have met many early Christians,
including the heretical Docetists, who did in fact deny the
reality of the suffering and death of God. The Docetists

explained that a phantom in his shape had been substituted for Jesus on Golgotha, and it was this that the soldiers had crucified. Muhammad adopted this story as his own revelation from God and in the Koran 4:157 writes that Jesus was not crucified but was taken up into heaven alive after another person who resembled him was killed in his place. According to Muhammad, not only did Jesus not die for human sin, Jesus did not even die.

At a later date, when Muhammad was fighting with the poor Christians of Arabia, the Koran added to these facts some anti-Christian polemics:

> The Christians were wrong in saying that Jesus, the superman was the son of Allah; Allah, being himself uncreated, could not create. They were wrong to believe in a Trinity made up of Allah, Jesus and Mary. There was only one God, Allah. Jesus himself had condemned these exaggerations and was quite innocent of them. Like his mother, he took food. He was not God.

Clearly Muhammad, or the one who revealed this truth to him, was confused about the makeup of the Christian Trinity.

Though hostile to the Jewish and Christian viewpoints, Muhammad taught that Jews and Christians were both "People of the Book" (*ahl alkitab*) and should be respected because God revealed himself to them. "When the revelations of the Merciful were recited to them, they fell down on their knees in tears and adoration. But the generations who succeeded them neglected their prayers and succumbed to temptation. These shall assuredly be lost" (Koran 19:53).

The point is that the Koran is one more ancient document that testifies to the historicity of Jesus. Though written several centuries after the time of Jesus, it does not doubt his existence or the fact that the Jews and Romans at least thought they had tried and executed someone named

Jesus. Muhammad does not accept the resurrection, but he does consider Jesus "to have eclipsed all Jewish prophets."[14]

*   *   *

All of these documents, though varying in reliability, can be used to establish, first of all, the fact that people genuinely believed in the existence of Jesus and the laws and traditions of his time. Second, while some of these sources directly contradict the Gospel accounts of the trial and death of Jesus, they are clearly propagandistic responses to the earlier Christian version of events.

Third, and perhaps most importantly, they can be used to test the general veracity of the Gospel versions themselves, for in every case, the Gospels prove to be the most thorough, credible, and reliable versions extant. As a group, they are largely consistent with each other, and contain none of the confusing inconsistencies found in these other versions. All this evidence, therefore, is submitted for our further analysis of the trial of Jesus.

chapter 6
THE APOCRYPHA

Another category of ancient source materials can be classified as *apocrypha,* a word that means "hidden or secret." The term has been applied to many ancient manuscripts by Jewish and Christian writers that have been discovered, translated, treasured, and studied over the centuries. Some of these materials claim to be orthodox Christian accounts of the trial and death of Jesus, but they are often heretical or misguided inventions.

When capitalized, *apocrypha* refers to the Jewish Apocrypha, which appeared between the periods of the Old and New Testaments. These fourteen books have been rejected from the canon by modern Jews, but the Roman Catholic Church has included them in their editions of the Bible since 1546. Most Protestant denominations reject the Apocrypha because the books were not quoted by Jesus or the apostles, or found in the authoritative ancient manuscripts of the Hebrew canon. Moreover, the writings have been described by scholars as "of inferior quality, not worthy of a place in the sacred scriptures."[1]

Our chief interest in this body of writing will be the book of

Susanna, one of the "traditional" stories of the Apocrypha, which are called "historical romances" by writer Isaac Asimov. Since the book of Susanna offers insight into the Jewish legal customs of the time, it will be discussed in detail in the next chapter on the "Hebrew Trial."

In this chapter I would like to focus on the Christian apocryphal literature. Among the earliest apocryphal writings, which were widely studied and treasured by Christians in the first three centuries A.D. are such works as the Acts of John, Paul, Peter, Andrew, and Thomas; the Gospels of the Infancy; the narratives of the Assumption of the Virgin; and the Descent into Hell. There is not adequate space to discuss the nature of all those books here. Suffice it to say that their style and intent clearly show them to be later mythological accretions to the orthodox body of Scripture. The story known as "Saint John and the Bedbugs" from the apocryphal Acts of John is a worthy example of the pietistic and often ludicrous stories found in many of these books:

> On the first day we arrived at a lonely inn; and while we were trying to find a bed for John we saw a curious thing. There was one bed there lying somewhere not made up; so we spread the cloaks which we were wearing over it, and begged him to lie down on it and take his ease, while all the rest of us slept on the floor. But when he lay down he was troubled by bugs, and as they became more and more troublesome to him, and it was already midnight, he said to them in the hearing of us all: "I tell you, you bugs, to behave yourselves, one and all; you must leave your home for tonight and be quiet in one place and keep your distance from the servants of God." And while we laughed and went on talking, John went to sleep; but we talked quietly and thanks to him were not disturbed.
>
> Now as the day was breaking I got up first, and Verus and Andronicus with me; and we saw by the

door of the room which we had taken a mass of bugs
had collected; and as we were astounded at the great
number of them, and all the brethren had woken up
because of them, John went on sleeping. And when he
woke up we explained to him what we had seen. And
he sat up in bed and looked at them and said, "Since
you have behaved yourselves and listened to my
correction, go back to your own place." And when he
had said this and had got up from the bed, the bugs
came running from the door toward the bed and
climbed up its legs and disappeared into the joints.
Then John said again, "This creature listened to a
man's voice and kept to itself and was quiet and
obedient; but we who hear the voice of God disobey
his commandments and are irresponsible; how long
will this go on?"[2]

This kind of anecdote, obviously, would not stand up
against Starkie's touchstones of reliability.

THE ACTS OF PILATE

One Christian apocryphal book is primarily about the trial
of Jesus. That is the Gospel of Nicodemus, often referred to
as the Acts of Pilate.[3] It is divided into two parts; the story of
the Passion and the Resurrection (written about A.D. 300),
and the Descent into Hell (added sometime after A.D. 400).
The first part was meant to prove that Jesus rose from the
dead and that Pilate found him innocent of any crime, yet
allowed the execution anyway. The second part was written
to prove that righteous Jewish fathers were delivered from
hell by the atoning death of Christ, a theme that was common
in some Christian writings as early as the second century A.D.

Since the Acts of Pilate contain the most extensive account
of the trial of Jesus anywhere outside the New Testament, the
relevant portions are quoted at length in Exhibit C in the

appendix. We must evaluate the Acts of Pilate in light of the
Gospel versions and ask such questions as: Are the facts
consistent? Are they believable? Is the tone of the prose
similar to that of the Gospels? What elements (if any) cast
doubt on its accuracy? What were the motives of the
supposed author, Nicodemus?

The Acts of Pilate contain miracles and mysteries, but
unlike those in the Gospel versions they do not ring true. For
instance, compare Jesus' interviews with Pilate as given in
the Gospel of John and the Acts of Pilate. In John, Pilate
summons Jesus and asks him who he is. The defendant
replies that he is a king but not of this world (John 18:33–37).
It is this exchange that leads to the famous inquiry by the
procurator, "What is truth?" The events seem believable and
well within the realm of human possibility.

But in the Acts of Pilate, Pilate's messenger, upon seeing
Jesus, worships him and calls him Lord, and then the carved
images on the Roman standards bow to Jesus. Even when
strong men are ordered to hold the standards upright, they
continue to bow. Pilate, of course, is frightened by this
supernatural display, and just then, his wife sends a messenger telling Pilate to have nothing to do with this "just man."
Yet even though Pilate witnesses such wonders, he allows
himself to be manipulated by the leaders of the Sanhedrin.
These events, by contrast, seem unbelievable.

Although portions of the Acts of Pilate are based on the
Gospels, the author has injected many unreasonable details,
such as a miraculous appearance of the twelve eyewitnesses
to Mary and Joseph's espousal. The storyline is too fantastic
to be a factual reporting by a simple follower of Jesus. The
book is not Scripture, but a novelette, written 300 years after
the fact, perhaps with good intentions but untrustworthy.

Yet this book, like much of the Christian apocrypha,
illuminates one important point: the Gospels are balanced and
credible by comparison. The Scriptures were gleaned with

great care from hundreds of competing manuscripts over the centuries. These documents were studied by Jews, Moslems, and Christians of all denominations.

THE EPISTLE OF BARNABAS

In many cases it is hard to distinguish between popular fable and outright propaganda. A good example is the Epistle of Barnabas. While the date and authorship is in doubt, many scholars believe the book was written in the fourteenth century by an Italian Christian who converted to Islam.[4] The book contains sections from both the Koran and the four Gospels, but it falls into the heresy of Docetism, the author being unwilling to accept the idea that Jesus, a prophet of God, could or should die for anyone's sins. The story claims that Jesus, with the help of angels, escaped from his trial through a window and that Judas, miraculously, "was so changed in speech and in face to be like Jesus" that the soldiers, priests, and Pilate were deceived and Judas was crucified in Jesus' place. The late date and the creatively outlandish theory presented in this book would seem to more than discredit this account.

If nothing else, the Gospel of Barnabas testifies to the fact that many people have been willing to corrupt the accounts of Jesus' life and trial for their own purposes. It has even been used for political purposes, as the legendary history of Joseph of Arimathea shows.

JOSEPH OF ARIMATHEA

Some critics of the apocrypha have difficulty distinguishing between the sincerely pious works and the manipulative propaganda, which is usually uninspired public relations. Jesus warned his followers to beware of false teachers and to rely on the Holy Spirit to discern the truth. Some ancient

writings are clearly political propaganda. A fascinating example is the legend of Joseph of Arimathea traveling to and
founding the Christian church in England shortly after the
trial of Jesus. Its political implications disqualify it from all
credibility, but it certainly must be placed alongside the other
bits of evidence concerning the trial, death, and resurrection
of Jesus.

The earliest written record of the fable comes from A.D. 314
when the Celtic church in Britain sent three bishops to the
Council of Arles. The original tale was simply that Joseph,
who had witnessed the trial of Jesus, later requested Christ's
body, donated the tomb, came to Glastonbury in England,
and founded an abbey. He was in a sense the first Christian
missionary to the native people of the British Isles.

The tale cannot be substantiated by even one piece of
evidence from the first century. What can be proven is that
the story took on a life of its own, and in the care of medieval
chroniclers and church politicians, it grew. By the fifteenth
century Joseph was not only a missionary, but the man who
brought to England the Holy Grail—that is, the cup that
Jesus passed around the table at the Last Supper. Hence,
Joseph becomes the father of England's ancestral fables of
King Arthur. Best of all, Joseph brought with him King
David's sword, "The most marvelous thing that ever forged
was," and it became the very sword that young Arthur
Pendragon pulled from a stone to then become king. We see
Christianity melting into Camelot. As the poet Alfred Lord
Tennyson wrote:

> From our old books I know
> That Joseph came of old to
> Glastonbury and there the heathen prince, Arviragus,
> Gave him an isle of marsh whereon to build
> A little lonely church in days of yore.[5]

Why is this fable relevant to this serious study of the trial? Because by 1431, the fable had been converted into "history." At the Council of Basle in 1431 the church fathers were fighting furiously over their pecking order. In many matters, from mere protocol such as seating, to weighty questions of theology, the antiquity of a nation's church was important. The debate between England and Spain was lengthy. Did the apostle James travel to Spain and establish the church before Joseph of Arimathea reached England? The Spaniards argued yes, but the English maintained that James was killed before ever reaching Spain and that the old abbey at Glastonbury was proof that Joseph did reach England. The bishops of London and Rochester drew up an affidavit or memorial to prove their case:

> . . . it is certain that in England, as may be ascertained from the very ancient books and archives, in particular the archives of the notable abbey of Glastonbury in the diocese of Bath, that Joseph of Arimathea, with twelve companions, was carried to England, escaping either from the persecution of Herod or from that of Roman high officials in Judaea. In that place (England) he preached what he had seen and heard of Christ; and so preaching he converted numberless English people. And from them he acquired many and countless things which were brought to him by those converted to the faith. These things he later left to a church of Christ erected by him at the time when Peter was preaching the faith at Antioch. The church built by Joseph became afterward the seat of a monastery with the rank of abbey and that noteworthy abbey and monastery has been preserved, praise to Christ himself, to this day.[6]

Historian Barbara Tuchman explains this miracle of fancy becoming fact, fiction turning into history:

The mainspring of the development of the Joseph legend lay in the ever-present British jealousy of Rome; in the urge to claim for the church in Britain an antiquity antedating that of Rome. In the person of Joseph, England's desire to bypass Rome and to trace the sources of its faith directly to the primary source in the Holy Land could be satisfied. Immediately after the Norman conquest the theory of a personal apostle to the Britons, a witness of, indeed an actor in, the drama of the crucifixion and resurrection, coming direct from Palestine to bring the word, first appears. Now everything Saxon was in its turn condemned by the Norman conquerors, while Celtic culture enjoyed a revival. The Arthurian cycle bursts into full bloom, transmuting the great champion of Celtic Britain and the knights of the Round Table into heroes of the age of chivalry. With it is entwined the legend of the quest for the Holy Grail, and into the leading role steps the one-time member of the Sanhedrin of Jerusalem, Joseph of Arimathea.[7]

Christian fact can easily become political fiction in the hands of people in the throes of religious or nationalistic fervor, a truth that we must be aware of in examining all of these conflicting accounts of Jesus' trial. We know Joseph was real. But the fable grew around him to fit the needs of its storytellers. How different are the Gospels and Paul's letters, which have not changed over time. As we discovered from the archaeological evidence, they have suffered no embellishment or added fictional narrative over the centuries.

LETTERS OF HEROD AND PILATE

Other apocryphal writings, although rejected by both Catholic and Protestant churches, are interesting in that they were often used by the early church for instruction. Consider the Letters of Herod and Pilate, written in Syria in the sixth or seventh century and now kept in the British Museum. The thrust of one letter allegedly from Herod is that he and his entire family suffered horrible punishments because he participated in the condemnation of Jesus. Pilate's reply confirms that Procula, his wife, and the twelve Roman soldiers who guarded the tomb witnessed the resurrected Christ. Pilate supposedly then went to Galilee with his wife and fifty Romans to verify for himself that Christ was alive. The letter states:

> And when we drew nigh to him, O Herod, a great voice was heard from heaven, and dreadful thunder, and the earth trembled, and gave forth a sweet smell, like unto which was never perceived even in the temple of Jerusalem. Now while I stood in the way, our Lord saw me as he stood and talked with his disciples. But I prayed in my heart, for I knew that it was he whom ye delivered unto me, that he was Lord of created things and Creator of all. But we, when we saw him, all of us fell upon our faces before his feet. And I said with a loud voice, I have sinned, O Lord, in that I sat and judged thee, who avengest all in truth. And lo, I know that thou art God, the Son of God, and I beheld thy humanity and not thy divinity.[8]

In other letters, Pilate wrote to Augustus Caesar and later to Tiberius to explain "what was done against Jesus by the Jews."[9] These letters affirm that Jesus was the Son of God and that Pilate was full of remorse for allowing Jesus to die. They place the blame squarely on the Jews who brought "many and endless allegations against him."[10]

The letters, of course, are nothing more than anti-Semitic propaganda, written over 500 years after the fact. What makes them fascinating is that some of the early church fathers believed them to be true, for in the Greek church, Procula is still considered a saint. The Ethiopian church considers both Procula and Pilate to be saints. The only biblical facts that could possibly support the idea that Pilate and his wife eventually believed in Christ are the incidents of Pilate washing his hands and Procula telling her husband to have nothing to do with this good man—hardly the stuff of sainthood. The only logical explanation for Saints Pilate and Procula is that some early powerful church leaders believed that the letters of Pilate were credible. They are, however, no more factual than the legend of King Arthur finding the sword of Joseph of Arimathea embedded in a rock.

EUSEBIUS

Eusebius was a Greek historian who lived from A.D. 260–339. A leading Christian scholar, he was twice imprisoned for his faith. He was appointed the bishop of Caesarea in A.D. 314 and held the post until his death. Of his forty-six books, fifteen have come down through the centuries intact.

His *History of the Church,* written between A.D. 310 and 324, focuses on the ideas of vengeance and divine justice, and gives us an accurate timeline by which to measure the span of Jesus' life. It also includes the dates for the appointments of the various emperors and priests. By reading his historical information, many of the events of the Gospels are supported and better understood. Although he has been both praised and criticized, the weight of expert opinion, as stated by Guy Schofield, is that he was "the dependable, the scholarly, the shrewd observer of the dubious . . . by far the most important and reliable historian of the ancient church."[11]

Eusebius is included in this chapter on Christian apocrypha, however, because of his transcription of the documents known as the "Letters from Edessa," written in Syriac, which he claims to have found in the Public Record Office in Edessa. These fascinating letters are allegedly a written request for a miracle by Jesus.

In A.D. 30, a prince from Edessa, a city located 180 miles

east of Antioch, wrote to Jesus. The prince, Abgar the Toparch, was in great physical pain, had heard of Jesus' miracles, and begged for healing. The letter and Jesus' written reply, transcribed and delivered by a courier named Ananias, are set out below:

Abgar Uchama the Toparch to Jesus, who has appeared as a gracious saviour in the region of Jerusalem—Greeting.

I have heard about you and about the cures you perform without drugs or herbs. If report is true, you make the blind see again and the lame walk about; you cleanse lepers, expel unclean spirits and demons, cure those suffering from chronic and painful diseases, and raise the dead. When I heard all this about you, I concluded that one of two things must be true—either you are God and came down from Heaven to do these things, or you are God's Son doing them. Accordingly, I am writing to beg you to come to me, whatever the inconvenience, and cure the disorder from which I suffer. I may add that I understand the Jews are treating you with contempt and desire to injure you: my city is very small, but highly esteemed, adequate for both of us.

Jesus' Reply to the Toparch Abgar by the Courier Ananias

Happy are you who believed in me without having seen me! For it is written of me that those who have seen me will not believe in me, and that those who have not seen will believe and live.* As to your request that I should come to you, I must complete all that I was sent to do here, and on completing it must at once be taken up to the One who sent me. When I have been taken up I will send you one of my disciples to cure

*John 20:29. Note resemblance of letter to phrases in John's gospel.

your disorder and bring life to you and those with you.[12]

To these letters is subjoined the following in Syriac:

After Jesus was taken up, Judas, also known as Thomas, sent to him as an apostle* Thaddaeus, one of the Seventy, who came and stayed with Tobias, son of Tobias. When his arrival was announced [and he had been made conspicuous by the wonders he performed], Abgar was told: "An apostle has come here from Jesus, as He promised you in His letter." Then Thaddaeus began in the power of God to cure every disease and weakness, to the astonishment of everyone . . . [Abgar replied] "Bring him to me." . . .

Thaddaeus answered: "I will present myself, since the power of God has sent me to him." [Abgar] questioned Thaddaeus. "Are you really a disciple of Jesus the Son of God, who said to me, 'I will send you one of my disciples who will cure you and give you life'?"

"You wholeheartedly believed in the One who sent me, and for that reason I was sent to you. And again, if you believe in Him, in proportion to your belief shall the prayers of your heart be granted."

"I believed in Him so strongly that I wanted to take an army and destroy the Jews who crucified Him, if I had not been prevented by the imperial power of Rome from doing so."

"Our Lord has fulfilled the will of His Father; after fulfilling it He was taken up to the Father."

"I too have believed in Him and in His Father."

"For that reason I lay my hand on you in His name."

*The word *apostle*, meaning "emissary," is not used in the narrow sense, but simply to denote any person sent by Christ.

> When he did this, Abgar was instantly cured of the disease and disorder from which he suffered. It surprised Abgar that the very thing he had heard about Jesus had actually happened to him through His disciple Thaddaeus . . .
> . . .So Abgar instructed his citizens to assemble at daybreak and hear the preaching of Thaddaeus. After that he ordered gold and silver to be given to him. But Thaddaeus refused them and asked, "If we have left our own property behind, how can we accept other peoples'?"[13]

These letters are not likely to contain the actual words of either Abgar or Jesus. While Eusebius probably did find them in the record office, these documents show, whether fiction, forgery, or fable, that Jesus' reputation as a miracle healer had spread far from his home in Palestine.

THE HERESIES

While the writings of Paul were accepted as orthodox teachings of Christian theology, in the first few centuries they were constantly in competition with other, often inconsistent teachings. These teachings were not based on fables, but on different interpretations of Christ's teachings. There were many heretical manifestations of Christian faith and dogma, including Pelagianism, Millenarianism, Quatrodecimans, Encratism, and Ebionism. Later orthodox Christian scholars such as Justin Martyr, Irenaeus, and others wrote critically of these heresies, which eventually vanished. Only the Pauline version of Christianity and its accompaniment of cultural practices survived with any force into the Middle Ages.

The most commonly recognized early heresy was Gnosticism. Proof of this ancient teaching was found in several scrolls uncovered in the famous dig at Nag Hammadi: The Apocrypha of John, the Apocalypse of Adam, and the Book

of the Great Seth. These have been referred to by the
prominent French Cardinal Jean Danielou, as "evidence of
this barely Christianized Jewish Gnosticism."[14] When the
philosopher Mani added his teaching to the Gnostic beliefs in
the third century, a larger religion—Manicheanism—grew
up. This faith was in direct competition not only with Pauline
Christianity, but with Zoroastrianism, the ancient religion of
Iran. Barbara Tuchman provides a succinct example of one of
the heresies that failed—Pelagianism:

> He was the British monk Pelagius, expounder of the
> celebrated heresy named after him, who came to the
> Holy Land about the year 413. He had been living in
> Rome until the sack of the city by Alaric the Goth
> forced him with many other residents to flee to
> Carthage. Pelagius, a man of untroubled faith, did not
> share the awful soul struggles of the Saint of Hippo,
> nor could he accept Augustine's insistence that salva-
> tion was not within man's power to achieve, but was
> only within the Divine power to bestow. Hoping to find
> a more sympathetic religious climate, he moved on to
> Palestine, only to come up against the cantankerous
> Jerome, who promptly denounced him as an old fool
> dulled by Scotch porridge (whiskey). For already his
> creed, contained in a series of commentaries on St.
> Paul, which incidentally form the oldest known book to
> have been written by a Briton, was making enemies for
> him among the entrenched episcopacy, in proportion
> as it gained headway in the Christian world . . .
>
> Repudiating the doctrine of original sin, he suggested
> instead that sin was a matter of choice rather than an
> unavoidable inheritance from Adam. This appalling
> theory filled church officials with horror. For if it were
> admitted that men were not totally depraved from birth
> but could achieve righteousness and grace through
> their own ability, then of what avail was Jesus'
> atonement on the Cross? If the Redeemer was not a

necessity for mankind, no more was the Church. Such
subversive ideas could not be allowed by the doctri-
naires of the day. Led by Augustine and Jerome, they
kept the controversy raging until they had secured the
condemnation of Pelagianism as heresy.[15]

Unlike these heresies, the Christian faith as taught by Paul
was to gain universal acceptance in the Hellenistic and
Roman world. It failed to make a great impact on the Middle
East and Asia, where the Judaeo-Christians, the Judaizers,
and all the myriad heresies either died out, reverted into the
orthodox Jewish faith, or melted into Islam.

We have only briefly touched on the thousands of source
materials available. These documents in addition to the many
religious teachings documented in thousands of ancient
writings, rock foundations of temples, and the cultural
evidence of communities throughout the world, support the
proposition that Jesus lived and taught in a real world.

The marketplace of ideas was as freewheeling in ancient
times as it is today. The message of Christ was interpreted by
many, and most of the peculiar additions were correctly
branded heresies and faded away. The basic message of
Christianity remains in the clear, simple words of the four
Gospels. Paul brought those truths out of the strict Jewish
cultural matrix and helped the faith become available to Jew
and Gentile alike. The human apocrypha, propaganda, and
fables that deviated from the truth were ground down slowly
but finely in the mills of time.

PART THREE
The Trials

chapter 7
THE HEBREW TRIAL

While it was still dark in the Garden of Gethsemane, Judas Iscariot led a band of Roman soldiers to the place where Jesus was praying. Surrounded by sleepy disciples, Jesus knew he must go peaceably. It was God's plan.

Suddenly awakened, some of the disciples wanted to fight, to protect their teacher. Peter struck swiftly. With his sword he cut off the ear of Malchus, the servant of the high priest. Christ commanded Peter to put his sword away; "Shall I not drink the cup the Father has given me?" (John 18:11). Then the guards tied Jesus' hands and led him to the house of Annas, the father-in-law of Caiaphas, the high priest.

AT THE HOUSE OF ANNAS

The interview with Annas cannot properly be called a trial, violating, as we shall see, the procedural rules of Jewish criminal law. But it lends credence to the accusation that the Jewish leaders never intended to give Jesus a formal trial. Or as John 11:53 puts it: "They plotted to take his life." They were no doubt hoping that Annas could elicit information that could be used against Jesus later.

John is the only Gospel to mention the hearing before Annas. Scholars suspect that if the Gospel is based on John's own recollections, then John himself may have been the only disciple to witness the events at the house of Annas. In that case, he is referring to himself in 18:15 when he says that both Peter and a "disciple . . . known to the high priest" followed Jesus into the courtyard of the high priest. It was there that Peter first denied Jesus.

Annas interrogated Jesus about his disciples and teachings. Jesus answered him truthfully, if perhaps a bit impudently: "I always taught in synagogues or at the temple, where all the Jews come together. I said nothing in secret. Why question me? Ask those who heard me. Surely they know what I said" (John 18:20–21).

Yet speaking forthrightly to the proud, self-righteous Annas was not permitted. An officer slapped Jesus across the face and said: "Is this the way you answer the high priest?" (18:22).

Now Jesus stood, his hands still tied, before the officer and the high priest, and he boldly invited another assault: "If I said something wrong . . . testify as to what is wrong. But if I spoke the truth, why did you strike me?" (18:23).

The significance of this scene is not in the evidence adduced, but in the further credibility it lends to the Gospel itself. Why would John alone mention this scene? Because he alone, of all the disciples, witnessed it. Peter was there, but he had to wait outside (18:16), warming himself by a fire and talking with bystanders who accused him of being a follower of Jesus (18:17, 25–26). John, however, was known to the high priest and was present at the interview. I imagine John later, as an old man, talking with his own followers about his recollections of that night in the courtyard of the high priest. He mentioned it not for any great spiritual lessons imparted by Christ's testimony before Annas, but simply because it happened. Even if the document is based on John's followers' recollections of his account, it is clearly a unique eyewitness testimony.

Jesus had either angered or frustrated Annas. No admissions of guilt had been obtained. No evidence was produced. Legally, the Jews were no further than they were before the arrest. Jesus had refused to play into their trap and even had the courage to ignore the jurisdiction of the court, knowing that the verdict would be handed down elsewhere.

The hearing was legally improper, being well outside the normal Jewish legal procedure. It could be compared to an inquisition, a variant of a grand jury proceeding where an inquisitor attempts to discover facts for use in a subsequent trial. Obviously, Annas failed. Having learned nothing in his questioning, he sent Jesus to the Sanhedrin.

THE GREAT SANHEDRIN

The Great Sanhedrin was composed of seventy-one men. As members of the most powerful body in Jewish theocracy, these men exercised legislative, judicial, and executive powers, and controlled education, government, and religion, but only insofar as they did not offend Rome.

The word *Sanhedrin* is derived from a Greek word implying both "legislative assembly" and "ecclesiastical council." Earlier it was known as the Council of Ancients and the Grand Council. In the second book of the apocryphal Maccabees it was called the "Gerasia," or senate.

Scholars dispute the origin of the body itself. One school of thought believes the original Sanhedrin was established by Moses in the wilderness (Numbers 11:16–17). Some scholars contend that there was in fact no Sanhedrin at the time of Jesus' crucifixion, the original group having been disbanded when the tribes of Israel entered the Promised Land. Other scholars say the Sanhedrin was disbanded in 30 B.C. but later resurfaced in response to the everpresent need to resolve disputes.

In spite of these contradictory opinions, it is undisputed that many minor Sanhedrins existed. These local courts could be established anytime a Jewish community of 120 families or more desired to set up a governing body of elders. These minor Sanhedrins served as courts, presiding over both civil and criminal cases, tax appeals, the management of schools, distribution of charity, and local law-making bodies. This Jewish system of justice was simple and democratic. Appeals from these local Sanhedrins could be taken to the two minor Sanhedrins in Jerusalem, then to the Great Sanhedrin in the same city—something like our appeals court system in the United States.

Whether this Great Sanhedrin was the same one that was founded in Old Testament times is beside the point. It is well-established that a legal body by that name existed in Jerusalem at the time. In a study written in the nineteenth century, French scholar M. LeMann identified forty of the seventy-one members of that Sanhedrin by cross-checking the Talmud, the histories of Josephus, and the New Testament. Here are sixteen character sketches from from Le-Mann's descriptive analysis:

> *Caiaphas,* high priest who presided over the Sanhedrin during the trial of Jesus. He was in office from A.D. 25–36, during the entire term of Pilate's administration.

> *Ananos,* father of five sons who subsequently assumed his office, and father-in-law of Caiaphas. He was out of office at the time of the trial of Jesus, but he continued to be consulted on matters of importance. He and his family were considered to be haughty, audacious, and cruel.

> *Eleazar,* eldest son of Ananos, was high priest for one year only, from A.D. 23–24.

Jonathan, son of Ananos, simple priest during the trial of Jesus, later assumed the title of high priest after Caiaphas was deposed in A.D. 37.

Theophilus, son of Ananos, simple priest who later became high priest in place of his brother Jonathan, who was deposed by Vitellius in A.D. 38.

Matthias, son of Ananos, simple priest who became high priest for two years, from A.D. 42–44, succeeding Simon Cantharus, who was deposed by King Herod Agrippa.

Ananus, son of Ananos, simple priest who became high priest after the death of the Roman governor, Portius Festus in A.D. 62. He was deposed after three months for having illegally condemned the apostle James to be stoned.

Eleazar, who succeeded his brother Joazar in A.D. 2 by King Archelaus. He was deposed a short time later.

Simon Cantharus, simple priest who was made high priest in A.D. 42 by King Herod Agrippa, being deposed a few months later.

Jesus ben Sie, high priest from A.D. 2–6, succeeding Eleazar.

Israel ben Phabi, high priest for nine years under Valerius Grattus, Pontius Pilate's predecessor.

John, simple priest, mentioned in the Acts of the Apostles.

Alexander, simple priest, also mentioned in Acts, and in the writings of Josephus, who notes that he was later made an Alabarch, or first magistrate of the Jews, in Alexandria. King Herod Agrippa asked of him and obtained the loan of two-hundred thousand pieces of silver.

Ananias ben Nebedeus, simple priest, later became
high priest from A.D. 48–54. He is mentioned in the
Acts and by Josephus, and is identified as one of the
people who informed the governor against Paul. He
was thought to be a glutton, the Talmud mentioning
three-hundred calves and casks of wine, and forty pair
of young pigeons being brought together for his
pleasure.

Helcias, simple priest, keeper of the treasury of the
Temple. He was probably the one who gave Judas the
thirty pieces of silver.

Sceva, one of the principal priests. He is mentioned in
the Acts concerning his seven sons, who gave themselves up to witchcraft.[1]

These, then, are just some of the personalities that made up
the Great Sanhedrin that was called to order early one spring
morning in approximately A.D. 30. Their purpose—to hear
the case against Jesus of Nazareth.

JUDICIAL QUALIFICATIONS of Sanhedrin

Ideally, the members of the Great Sanhedrin were chosen
with careful regard to their qualifications. Judges were
supposed to be men of great wisdom and moderation, pious,
of good character, learned in the law, and with practical
experience. Members had to be accomplished in both science
and linguistics, since no interpreters were allowed in court. In
the polyglot and cosmopolitan capital of Jerusalem, these
men had to be highly educated and sophisticated.

A man could be disqualified from the Sanhedrin if he lacked
an occupation, for members were not compensated for their
services. Like judges today, the Sanhedrin wished to avoid
even the appearance of impropriety. With every member
gainfully employed, there could be no hint of bribery or self-
advancement. For this reason a member could be disqualified

from judging any case in which he had a conflict of interest.
Gamblers were disqualified, for that reason, and in capital
offense cases, elderly or childless members were disqualified
as being without adequate empathy for the accused.

As you can see from the brief biographies above, the
members of the Great Sanhedrin in Jerusalem did not rise to
the level of excellence that was required. They bowed to
nepotism and could be swayed by money and personal
interest. The Talmud, in Pesachim, folio 57, speaks sorrow-
fully of this sacrilege:

> What a plague is the family of Simon Boethus; cursed
> be their lances! What a plague is the family of Ananos;
> cursed be their hissing of vipers! What a plague is the
> family of Cantharus; cursed be their pens! What a
> plague is the family of Ismael ben Phabi; cursed be
> their fists! They are high priests themselves, their sons
> are treasurers, their sons-in-law are commanders, and
> their servants strike the people with staves.

In addition, though they may have understood the laws and
rules of their office, they violated their own procedures and
gave in to public pressure in the matter of the *People v. Jesus
of Nazareth, also known as Jesus, the Christ.*

THE PROCEDURES

The sessions of the Sanhedrin were convened whenever a
case was presented. A summons went out after the morning
sacrifice, and normally most sessions ended at noon. A case
could continue into the afternoon, but all criminal cases that
could not be concluded by the evening sacrifice had to be
continued the next day. The rules clearly stated that it was
illegal for any criminal proceeding to take place at night—the
first of many procedural errors in the trial of Jesus.

The sessions of the Sanhedrin commenced when a quorum

of twenty-three members had gathered. No lawyers or advocates represented the accused. The complainant brought the accusation, and additional witnesses were necessary to support the claimed wrong. Like our modern system of justice, the Sanhedrin presumed the accused to be innocent and used many legal procedures to protect the accused. In some ways, the system was far more protective of the rights of the accused than even our U.S. Supreme Court during the years Earl Warren was Chief Justice. Some of the procedures of the Sanhedrin encouraged an actual bias in favor of the accused. For instance, one maxim from the Mishnah (the oral law of the Talmud) stated, "The Sanhedrin that executes more than one man in seven years is a slaughterhouse."

Nor could a conviction be enforced unless strict rules of procedure were followed. Our own *Miranda* decision, which requires a police officer to inform a suspect of his or her Constitutional rights, is a relatively simple matter when compared with the Sanhedrin's myriad of procedural protections. While a majority of one could support a finding of acquittal, a conviction required a majority of two. Even more surprising is the Sanhedrin's rule that states: "A simultaneous and unanimous verdict of guilty rendered on the day of trial had the effect of an acquittal."[2] This rule illustrates the inherent distrust of mob rule and the overriding principle of mercy. Since there were no public prosecutors, the accuser became the advocate for society. The accused criminal was often defended by the members of the Sanhedrin itself. Walter Chandler, a lawyer and expert on the trial of Jesus, observed: "Judges were the defenders as well as the judges of the accused."[3]

When a defendant was convicted of a capital crime, a dramatic scene followed. The accuser, not the court, had the responsibility of executing the guilty party. This method of meting out punishment stands in stark contrast to the prohibition of allowing individual judges to decide cases. The

Turn page

Christ Before Caiaphas. After an unattributed painting. Presumably the two men in the background are the witnesses who claimed to have overheard Jesus' words about destroying the temple and rebuilding it in three days. The scene captures the dramatic moment just before Caiaphas stands up and tears his robes.

Jews believed it would be an affront to God if a single man sat in judgment of another. "Be not a sole judge, for there is no sole judge but One."[4]

These facts are necessary for a true understanding of the trial. He was accused by the chief priests of blasphemy, but none of them wanted the responsibility of being an accuser and, thereby, individual executioner. The role of Pilate, therefore, becomes all the more significant. The Jews wanted him to exercise his judicial prerogative. The consciences of many of the Jewish bystanders must therefore have been troubled when Pilate washed his hands, for he was, in essence, stating that he was neither the accuser nor the executioner of Jesus. By that action, he placed the responsibility back on the Sanhedrin.

LEGAL ERRORS

Did the Sanhedrin mistakenly convict an innocent man? Or did they intentionally overlook the legal irregularities to be rid of Jesus? The fact is, the trial as recounted in all four Gospels falls far short of the legal procedures established by the Jewish legal system itself. At least nine specific errors were made. Examine them carefully and ask yourself whether they were harmless errors:

1. *Witnesses.* Two witnesses were needed for conviction in Jewish trials, a requirement based on the Mosaic and Talmudic law (Numbers 35:30). When the prosecuting or accusing witness (similar to the plaintiff in modern trials) was included, the law required three people to give specific examples of crime. The record shows that this burden of proof was not met in the case of Jesus. According to Matthew 26:60, only two witnesses (false ones at that) came forward. No prosecuting witness is mentioned. Although Mark says that "many" witnesses came forward, neither does he mention any prosecuting witness. After this exchange, the

chief priest asked Jesus if he was the Son of God, to which
Jesus answered, "You are right in saying I am" (Luke 22:70).
Jesus' words were immediately used against him. The high
priest then tore his robes after hearing what he considered
blasphemy from Jesus' lips. "Why do we need any more
testimony? We have heard it from his own lips" (Luke 22:71;
also Mark 14:63). In this case, no witnesses were called at all.
The chief priest improperly assumed the judges themselves
could serve as witnesses to an alleged crime they were
currently judging.

2. Consistency. The witnesses must concur on all essential
details. The testimony of all witnesses will be rejected if they
contradict each other. This principle is admittedly strange
and seemingly unworkable in our system. Yet it was applied
originally to criminal cases to protect the innocent; circumstantial evidence was not permitted. If this had been enforced
in Jesus' trial, then the witnesses would have been required
to recount, without contradiction, what events took place in
the temple where Jesus allegedly blasphemed. According to
the Gospels, this did not happen. Mark notes that they did not
agree on the details.

3. Protection of witness testimony. According to Jewish
law, witnesses should be sequestered. The practice of
separating witnesses is still often used today in criminal
cases. This helps prevent conspiracies to defraud the court.
As this was essential to Jesus' defense, and the Gospel
writers assert that the chief priest had obtained false witnesses, it seems obvious that the judicial body did not take
proper precautions to prevent witness tampering. After the
first false witnesses presented their accusations, states Mark
14:57–58, "some stood up and gave this false testimony
against him: 'We heard him say, "I will destroy this man-
made temple and in three days will build another, not made
by man." ' " In other words, the second group of witnesses
had been allowed to overhear the first group. You can feel the

irony in Mark's tone when he adds: "Yet even then their testimony did not agree" (Mark 14:59).

4. *Defendant inquiries.* The accused must be given an opportunity to cross-examine and confront his accusers. This was divided into two modes of examination, the *hakiroth* and the *bedikoth*. The *hakiroth* is related to our modern defense called *alibi*. If a defendant can prove that he was at a different place at the time of the crime, then he cannot have committed the crime. When Jesus was accused of being in the temple blaspheming God, he should have been given an opportunity to confront his accusers and ask them to specify exactly when the blasphemy occurred and what was said. If they convinced the Sanhedrin that Jesus did not have an alibi, then Jesus still could question the accusers under the *bedikoth*. This broader scope of examination allows the accused to inquire as to all relevant facts supporting the accuser's story.

5. *Self-incrimination.* The accused was never compelled to testify against himself, as the high priest's question forces Jesus to do. This rule is similar to our Fifth Amendment right against self-incrimination. A related rule was that the accused would be encouraged to offer testimony on his own behalf. Arguably, Jesus waived this right when he told Caiaphas that he was the "Son of Man," repeating in the presence of all the judges the blasphemy of which he was accused (Mark 14:62). Of course, since Christians believe he really was the Son of Man, it was not blasphemy at all but Jesus' honest declaration of his Father's plan.

6. *Illegal confession.* Even if we assume Jesus did admit to uttering words that the Jews believed were blasphemous, that is not a confession to the crime of blasphemy. A crime is defined as an act coupled with an intention that is outside the law. If Christ spoke and blasphemed God it would be a crime, unless the statement was true. All those Christians who believe that Jesus was the true Son of God must agree that Jesus did not commit blasphemy.

7. *Antecedent warning.* The evidence failed to show that
antecedent warning of the crime was given to Jesus. This last
legal argument is based upon a seemingly absurd provision in
the Jewish law. It applied to criminal cases only, and one
wonders whether any criminal could have been convicted
under the strict interpretation of the rule. The rule states:
"No person charged with a crime involving life and death, or
even corporal punishment, could be convicted, unless it was
shown by competent testimony, that immediately before the
commission of the crime the offender was warned that what
he was about to do was a crime, and that a certain penalty
was attached thereto." The purpose of this incredible ruling
was to prevent an ignorant or rash act from ruining the life of
a child of God. This rule was established by the Talmudic law
and several crimes were excepted, including bearing false
witness, worshiping idols, and burglary, none of which
applied to the case against Jesus.

8. *Arguments.* The debate following the testimony, in
which the high priest directed the meeting, violated the rules
of procedure. In a capital case the debate started with the
youngest judge so as not to intimidate the youthful or shy.
Debate must begin with the argument defending the accused
and then, after all arguments in defense of the accused are
exhausted, lead on to the prosecution. Each ballot must be
cast in the proper order and then followed by oral arguments.
Balloting continued until a majority of one favored acquittal
or a majority of two favored conviction. Once a vote for
conviction was cast, however, it could always be withdrawn
and cast as a vote for acquittal. Once a vote for acquittal was
cast, it could never be changed to conviction. The records
available show no proper balloting or discussion. Caiaphas
shouted that Jesus had confessed: "Why do we need any
more witnesses? . . . You have heard the blasphemy. What
do you think?" (Mark 14:63–64). Caiaphas rent his clothes,
the traditional Jewish response to blasphemy, as either a

righteous man or a shrewd trial attorney would do under the circumstances. We see a dramatic display of righteous indignation coupled with a plea for punishment. We do not see a serious group of elders deliberating according to law.

9. *Execution.* The death sentence was carried out on the same day as the conviction. According to Jewish law an actual execution must never be carried out before sunset of the following day. This delay was designed to prevent mob action and to allow the judges additional time to pray and discuss the facts. This had the character of an appeal phase. The judges were left to meditate and were not allowed heavy food or intoxicants. The night of a conviction the judges were expected to meet in their homes in small groups and confer. Even if no new evidence was discovered, they reconvened the next morning after prayers and reopened the case. This preoccupation with fairness continued right through the death march. The convicted criminal even had the right to stop the death march five times and return to the judgment hall. Every time the procession was postponed all passersby were asked if they knew of any new evidence that should be considered.

CROSS-EXAMINATION

In any trial where the judges really want to find the truth, it is essential to question the witnesses. Many times in criminal trials today the witnesses are prohibited from sitting in the courtroom while another witness is testifying. The obvious protection is to prevent one witness from merely imitating the testimony of another. We know from Jewish literature that this cross-examination stage of witnesses, and the practice of sequestering witnesses, was in common practice even before the trial of Jesus.

The best example of the usefulness of cross-examination is from the apocryphal "Susanna and the Elders." This story was written down long before Jesus' time, and its theme,

virtue triumphant over evil, is set in the context of, first, a
sham trial put on by a corrupt judiciary, and then a second,
valid trial where the truth comes out only by vigorous cross-
examination and sequestered witnesses. Here is a condensed
version of that famous Jewish story.[5]

Susanna and her husband, Joacim, lived in Babylon. She
had been raised by the law of Moses and was a God-fearing
woman. Joacim was wealthy and respected, and had a
beautiful garden adjoining his house.

At that time two of the ancients of the people, or "elders,"
were appointed to be judges. They frequented Joacim and
Susanna's house; and all that had any suits in law came to
them.

After the people left at noon, Susanna had a habit of
walking in the garden. The two elders saw her going there,
and lusted after her. They were ashamed of these emotions,
but continued to watch her day after day. Finally they
confessed their lust to one another, and then decided to find
her alone.

On one hot afternoon, Susanna was in the garden bathing.
The elders were watching her as usual, and when she sent her
maids away for a moment to shut the doors and bring her oil
and washing balls, the elders approached her.

Now when the maids had gone, the two elders got up and
ran unto her, saying, "Behold, the garden doors are shut, that
no man can see us, and we are in love with thee; therefore
consent unto us, and lie with us. If thou wilt not, we will bear
witness against thee, that a young man was with thee: and
therefore thou didst send away thy maids from thee."

Susanna, understanding the consequences, decided she
would rather face their accusations than stoop to fornication.
She screamed, calling the servants to her, and the elders ran
out. The elders made their accusation, and she was brought
to trial the next day.

The two elders told their lies at Susanna's trial, as Susanna kept her eyes toward heaven, trusting in God. The elders explained that they had tried to hold the man they had seen in Susanna's garden, but he had escaped. And when they asked Susanna, she would not tell them a thing. The assembly believed these elders, and condemned Susanna to death.

Then Susanna cried out in a loud voice, "O everlasting God, that knowest the secrets, and knowest all things before they be: thou knowest that they have borne false witness against me, and, behold, I must die: whereas I never did such things as these men have maliciously invented against me." And the Lord heard her voice.

Therefore when she was about to be put to death, the Lord caused a young man, by the name of Daniel to speak out boldly, "I am clear from the blood of this woman."

The people then turned toward him and said, "What mean these words that thou hast spoken?"

So while he stood among them he said, "Are ye such fools, ye sons of Israel, that without examination or knowledge of the truth ye have condemned a daughter of Israel? Return again to the place of judgment: for they have borne false witness against her."

Daniel was invited to sit with the assembly as an elder, and he instructed them to separate the witnesses. Then he called them one at a time and asked them under what tree they had seen Susanna with the young man. The first elder replied, "Under the mastic tree." The second, who had been kept apart from the first during questioning, said, "Under a holm tree."

As Daniel condemned them for their lies, the assembly praised God for this miracle; then they took the two elders and put them to death.

*   *   *

Even if the Sanhedrin considered itself the witnesses of Jesus' supposed blasphemy, which of course would have been illegal because they should never have judged cases in which they were witnesses, Jesus was still not accorded the right to hear all the witnesses' testimonies, nor were the witnesses sequestered from each other and cross-examined separately as the law required.

My conclusion is that Jesus of Nazareth was not accorded the rights due him under the Jewish trial law of the time. He was considered a threat to the material wealth and religious peace of the Sanhedrin. My chief witness is the apostle John who concluded that the chief priests and scribes had conspired to deny Jesus a fair trial and put him to death.

THE CHARGE

So what specific charge was brought against Jesus under Jewish law? The charge was religious, that Jesus had committed blasphemy. But what exactly had he done that was blasphemous?

The ostensible charge was that Jesus had prophesied the destruction of the temple; yet even the Old Testament prophets often spoke of that event as inevitable. Jesus, the high priest might have argued, went a step further. He had said that he had the power to destroy and then to rebuild it in three days. This was certainly an outrageous claim, but was it blasphemous? It was never argued at the trial.

Earlier, Jesus had said, "Before Abraham was born, I am" (John 8:58), referring to God, who called himself "I am." When Jesus was asked about his Sabbath healing, he had answered, "As long as it is day, we must do the work of him who sent me" (John 9:4). In the temple, he had said, "I and the Father are one." To the zealously monotheistic Jews such a claim was blasphemous. For this reason they also accused him of blasphemy when he forgave the paralytic for his sins (Mark 2:7), for only God can forgive sin.

These incidents may have been in the minds of the

members of the Sanhedrin, yet no honest witnesses were called. Caiaphas merely tore his robes when Jesus ambiguously referred to the "Son of Man," and Caiaphas stated that no other witnesses were needed. There is some dispute about the actual meaning of the phrase, "Son of Man." Some scholars insist that it is the same as "Son of God," a claim that every Jew could make because all Jews were the special children of God. Yet the Jews of the time must have seen it differently. To them the phrase meant "the Messiah," the chosen one of God. John 19:7 quotes the Jews as saying, "We have a law, and according to that law he must die, because he claimed to be the Son of God."

Jesus' explicit statement at the trial—that "you will see the Son of Man sitting at the right hand of the Mighty One"— might have appeared blasphemous; yet Jesus was careful to make it clear that God would announce this enthronement. This same care to avoid blasphemous statements is evident in his actions following John the Baptist's query (Matthew 11:2–4) and in Jesus' refusal to grant seats of honor in heaven to his disciples.

Any man who falsely claimed to be the Messiah was guilty of blasphemy; the punishment was death. The blasphemy is not in the title, but in the temerity of implying equality with God before he "had announced the enthronement of his anointed one." But here is where the charge against Jesus ultimately fails. Such a claim can only be blasphemous if it is untrue. This, of course, is exactly what the Sanhedrin could never have accepted, but it is what the foundation upon which all of Christianity is built: the divinity of Christ.

"WHO DO YOU SAY THAT I AM?"

This central question, asked of his disciples by Jesus, is the climax of Mark 8:29. At last Peter realizes that Jesus is the

Messiah, the Son of God. William Barclay has written a
thoughtful summary of "Who Jesus Was":

> **Messiah.** The Church affirmed immediately after the
> Resurrection that Jesus was the promised Messiah
> (Acts 2:36). Yet, when we turn to the Gospels we find
> that in the first three, although the word occurs fairly
> often, it is never ambiguously used by Jesus as a title
> for Himself. This is true, in slightly lesser degree, in
> John. He was conscious of a special relationship with
> God and a special mission which He must fulfill (cf. the
> voice at the Baptism) but He allowed the title to be
> ascribed to Him only with hesitation and unwillingness
> (when Peter confessed that He was the Christ, Jesus
> immediately enjoined silence).
>
> **Son of Man.** Jesus found for Himself a substitute
> title, Son of man, which He frequently used, as all the
> Gospels attest. It is reasonably safe to conclude that
> the name "expresses the idea of lordship, of rule over
> the Messianic community," and its associations are
> supernatural. It embodies His conception of Messiah-
> ship as the more familiar names could not do. . . .
> Even so the Son of man concept is not wide and rich
> enough to express what Jesus believes concerning His
> person and His work. That is why He re-interprets the
> idea in terms of the Suffering Servant, teaches that the
> Son of man must suffer, and in this persuasion goes
> deliberately to Jerusalem to die, convinced that He is
> fulfilling the purpose of His Father, with which He has
> completely identified Himself.
>
> **Son of God.** Did Jesus speak of Himself, or even
> think of Himself, thus? The answer is a clear
> affirmative. In the first three Gospels the title "Son of
> God" is given by the voice at the Baptism and the
> Transfiguration, and Jesus Himself was conscious of
> such a special relationship (see Matthew 11:25-27
> paralleled in Luke 10:22 and the parable of the
> vineyard tenants in Mark 12, etc.). In the fourth

Gospel the title occurs more often and in line with
John's particular emphases. In an intimate sense, too,
He spoke of "my Father."[6]

Jesus took care not to blaspheme. He did not immediately
announce his coming as the long-expected Messiah. He
awaited God's timing to inform the world. But he did admit
he was more than just a man, a rabbi, a prophet. The
ambiguity of his carefully worded replies infuriated the
Sanhedrin. Jesus was condemned, falsely, for equating
himself with God (John 10:33) by presuming to say he was the
Son when the Father alone knew who the Son was (Matthew
11:27; Luke 10:22). Jesus was innocent but was put to death
for the sins of the nation. Unknowingly the priests fulfilled
prophecy. In a way they never could have imagined, they
carried out the will of God.

chapter 8
THE ROMAN TRIAL

From what history tells us, Pontius Pilate was vain, cunning, and foolish. He offended his subjects repeatedly, endangered the fragile peace of the region, and authorized the crucifixion of Jesus of Nazareth, the Christ. He must have been a shrewd military man and a fairly clever politician, for no novice could have risen to the level of power he possessed in the Roman Empire. By looking at the Roman historical sources, we can better comprehend the reasons for Pilate's arrogance, and in hindsight see that he completely misunderstood the significance of this trial.

PILATE AND THE JEWS

Several years before the trial of Jesus, Pilate had made a major political blunder. He offended the Jews by bringing carved images of Caesar into Jerusalem, an act that violated the most basic Jewish law prohibiting idols. The ancient Jewish scholar Josephus reports what historians refer to as "The Case of the Standards":

Pilate, being sent by Tiberius as procurator to Judea, introduced into Jerusalem by night and under cover the effigies of Caesar which are called standards. This proceeding, when day broke, aroused immense excitement among the Jews; those on the spot were in consternation, considering their laws to have been trampled under foot, as those laws permit no image to be erected in the city; while the indignation of the townspeople stirred the country folk, who flocked together in crowds. Hastening after Pilate to Caesarea, the Jews implored him to remove the standards from Jerusalem and to uphold the laws of their ancestors. When Pilate refused, they fell prostrate around his house and for five whole days and nights remained motionless in that position.

On the ensuing day Pilate took his seat on his tribunal in the great stadium, and summoning the multitude with the apparent intention of answering them, gave the arranged signal to his armed soldiers to surround the Jews. Finding themselves in a ring of troops, three deep, the Jews were struck dumb at this unexpected sight. Pilate, after threatening to cut them down if they refused to admit Caesar's images, signaled to the soldiers to draw their swords. Thereupon the Jews, as by concerted action, flung themselves in a body on the ground, extended their necks, and exclaimed that they were ready to die rather than to transgress the Law. Overcome with astonishment at such religious zeal, Pilate gave orders for the immediate removal of the standards from Jerusalem.[1]

Pilate was stubborn, however, and tried again. According to Philo, a Roman historian, Pilate hung votive shields dedicated to Emperor Tiberius in Herod's palace. The Sanhedrin learned of it and sent a deputation that included all four of Herod's surviving sons. At first, Pilate refused to remove the shields. But the sons of Herod had power, and they appealed directly to Caesar in Rome. Tiberius sent a stern order to Pilate to move the shields from Jerusalem to Caesarea where they were hung in the temple of Augustus, the former emperor.

Another example of Pilate's insensitivity was the design he chose for the local coins at that time. Before A.D. 29 Pilate used a copper coin with a *lituus* on one side. The *lituus* was a staff of a pagan priest that was offensive to the Jews, a symbol of a false religion that they had to carry in their purses and use to buy their everyday needs. Unlike Pilate, his forerunners had used either stacks of wheat or palm branches on the official coins.

Through all this Pilate jousted with the Jews, underestimating their revulsion of idolatry and their united zeal when confronted with Roman blasphemy. On one occasion, he determined not to be defeated by the Jews he now hated and despised. The following passage, written by Josephus, recounts the strategy of Pilate and sets the stage for his arrogant hypocrisy during the trial of Jesus:

> On a later occasion, he provoked a fresh uproar by expending upon the construction of an aqueduct the sacred treasure known as corbonas. The water was brought from a distance of 400 furlongs. Indignant at this proceeding, the populace formed a ring around the tribunal of Pilate, then on a visit to Jerusalem, and besieged him with angry clamor. He, foreseeing the tumult, had interspersed among the crowd a troop of his soldiers, armed, but disguised in civilian dress, with orders not to use their swords, but to beat any rioters with cudgels. From his tribunal he gave the agreed signal. Large numbers of the Jews perished, some from the blows which they received, others trodden to death by their companions in the ensuing flight. Cowed by the fate of the victims, the multitude was reduced to silence.[2]

Eusebius follows this story with another:

> Besides this, the same writer shows that in Jerusalem itself a great many other revolts broke out, making it clear that from then on the city and all Judea were in the grip of faction, war, and an endless succession of criminal plots, until the final hour overtook them—the siege under Vespasian. . . .
>
> It is worthy of note that, as the records show, in the reign of Gaius, whose times I am describing, Pilate himself, the governor of our Saviour's day, was involved in such calamities that he was forced to become his own executioner and to punish himself with his own hand: divine justice, it seems, was not slow to overtake him. The facts are recorded by those Greeks who have chronicled the Olympiads together with the events occurring in each.[3]

The Roman governor had chosen brute force to subjugate the Jews. But his own position was now becoming perilous. When Jesus was brought before him, Pilate could not afford another loss of face with the Jews. This ironic shifting of power from Pilate back to the Jewish leaders is a cogent lesson in politics of the Roman Empire.

Pilate was originally appointed prefect in A.D. 26 at the request of Aelius Seianus, a high ranking Roman of great influence with Emperor Tiberius. Pilate's job was to keep the rebellious peoples of the far eastern edge of the Roman Empire at peace. Despite his blunders he remained a favorite of the emperor's. But in A.D. 31, Aelius Seianus himself was caught plotting to overthrow Tiberius. Pilate, a thousand miles away in Jerusalem, had no part in the scheme, but a cloud of suspicion descended on him. Since Pilate had no powerful protector in Rome to speak well of him to the emperor, he was in grave danger. It is not surprising that he tried to honor Tiberius with the standards and votive shields.

Christ Before Pilate. This scene, carved on an ancient stone sarcophagus, shows Jesus (at left) and Pilate (at right) washing his hands.

He was not wise enough to see that those attempts to appease the emperor would only create civil unrest and further weaken his position. He apparently feared the Jews less than he feared the emperor.

PILATE AND JESUS

So Jesus presented something of a political problem for Pilate. As a Jew from Galilee, Jesus was subject, in theological matters, to the Mosaic Law and Jewish teachings. In civil matters, however, he was subject to both the Tetrarch Herod Antipas and to Pilate himself. Which court had the power to try Jesus? The Sanhedrin? Herod's court? Or the Roman procurator's? In Jesus' case, all three had jurisdiction, and in fact, all three did exercise some power. Which court should have tried Jesus? For his accusers, the punishment was the deciding factor.

The Jews had found Jesus guilty of blasphemy, which was punishable by death. Although there is some disagreement *double charge (one for each court) shows intent.*

over whether the Jews had the authority to impose a death sentence during that period, according to New Testament sources they could not. The implication is that they went to Pilate not to obtain a just civil trial, but to request that Jesus be crucified. To achieve this, the Jews accused Jesus of perverting the nation and prohibiting tribute to Caesar— crimes against Rome, not blasphemy, the charges they had brought against him in the religious court.

Pilate heard the evidence and knew he was in a difficult position. When he learned that Jesus was from Galilee, he had an idea. While he had jurisdiction over Judea, Galilee was in Herod's realm. Pilate sent Jesus to Herod. By doing so, he thought he could avoid a difficult political situation and smooth over his already uneasy relationship with Herod and the Jews. But the solution failed. Thinking Jesus was a mere curiosity, Herod insisted on seeing a miracle (Luke 23:8). When Jesus refused, Herod sent him back to Pilate.

Jesus was then marched, hands tied, through the streets of Jerusalem to the Fortress of Antonia, the Roman military headquarters. In a courtyard beneath its tower, Jesus stood and waited. The trial itself was probably held in the Lithostratom, a courtyard of huge flagstones, three feet square and one foot thick, which provided support for the pillars and arches of the fortress. Some of the large stones were carved into game boards for the Roman troops stationed at the Antonia. The casting of lots for Jesus' lost possessions (John 19:23–24) may very well have been done on a stone diagram carved into the Lithostratom floor.

Pilate arrived and began his inquiry. The questions were few, brief, and not altogether relevant. The trial seemed to be over in a matter of minutes. Was this the extent of the civil trial of Jesus of Nazareth? According to the Gospels, it was. Was the dialogue ended so quickly or was there more that escaped the authors of the Gospels? Of course it is likely that few of Jesus' disciples, if any, were present at the Roman

Christt Before Pilate. After a sixteenth-century original by
Gaudenzio Farrari. While the people shout, "Crucify him!"
Pilate washes his hands as a ritual denial of responsibility.

trial, although the questioning may have been on a balcony overlooking the public square, which would allow some of Jesus' followers to overhear. In any case, we have a glimpse into the trial, even if we cannot know if the Gospel writers heard the words themselves or recorded the testimonies of those who did.

We know enough about this trial, however, to know it was unusual and improper. Let us turn to the classic Roman civil procedure to see what should have occurred. A Roman trial consisted of four elements: *indictment, examination, defense,* and *verdict*. An indictment was brought when someone was in violation of a Roman law. The indictment was usually presented by a prosecutor and signed by witnesses on a document called the *inscriptio*. The written charges were presented and a trial date set, affording ample time for both sides to gather evidence, which was called the *nominus receptio*. The first appearance of the accused in court was the *citatio*. The trial itself was always held in daylight. The prosecutor would read the charges and then question witnesses. The accused could be questioned by either prosecutor or judge. Then the accused could call witnesses on his behalf. At the close of evidence each side could argue and present illustrations to prove their case.

According to the Gospels, the political charges against Jesus were spoken, not presented in writing. This may have been because the Sanhedrin was merely seeking a confirmation of its own death sentence and not expecting formal trial from the Romans. Whatever their motives, Pilate, as a Roman magistrate, was unwilling to rubber-stamp their decision. He wanted to examine Jesus himself, so he moved directly to the *citatio* mode, that is, calling the accused to appear. Pilate asked the Jews what charges they had brought against Jesus; that is the *inscriptio* phase. They replied that they wanted Jesus put to death by crucifixion, an answer that implied that they did not want a trial, that justice was not their goal.

Matthew emphasizes the reluctance of Pilate to order such an execution: "While Pilate was sitting on the judge's seat, his wife sent him this message: 'Don't have anything to do with that innocent man, for I have suffered a great deal today in a dream because of him'" (Matthew 27:19). This is the only appearance of Claudia Procula, Pilate's wife, in the New Testament, though there is some evidence that she later became a secret Christian. She was, in fact, canonized by the Greek Orthodox Church.

Having offered to release Jesus, Pilate was faced with a continued cry for the execution. He protested: "What crime has he committed?" (Matthew 27:23).

The cry continued. Then, "when Pilate saw that he was getting nowhere, . . . he took water and washed his hands in front of the crowd. 'I am innocent of this man's blood,' he said. 'It is your responsibility!'" (Matthew 27:24). Isaac Asimov once wrote, "The four Gospels agree that Pilate was reluctant to order the execution of Jesus, but only Matthew inserts this hand-washing—a dramatic act that makes the English phrase 'to wash one's hands of' mean 'to disclaim responsibility.'"

It is an intriguing but unprovable theory that Pilate may have intentionally been imitating a traditional Jewish ritual when he washed his hands. In Deuteronomy it is stated that if a murdered body is found and the murderer is not known, the people of the nearest town go through a certain ritual, absolving themselves of guilt: "All the elders of the town nearest the body shall wash their hands over [a] heifer . . . and they shall declare: 'Our hands did not shed this blood'" (Deuteronomy 21:6–7).

Since Pilate thus proclaims his innocence, Matthew has the impatient crowd accept the responsibility themselves, making use of the dramatic Old Testament idiom used for that purpose: "All the people answered, 'Let his blood be on us and on our children'" (Matthew 27:25).

Pilate and Herod represented the highest civil courts in the region. Jesus could appeal to no higher earthly tribunal. Unlike Paul, Jesus was not a Roman citizen and could not therefore appeal to Caesar in Rome. A lowly carpenter, an itinerant teacher, an alleged troublemaker, he had a right to only one day in court. And yet, amazingly, Pilate found no fault in him. Pilate wanted to let him go.

These two powerful men, Herod and Pilate, had been enemies until that day, but their complicity in the crucifixion of Jesus made them friends (Luke 23:12). Both men, as judges in courts of law, found Jesus had committed no crime. Professor J. I. Packer, in his book *I Want to Be a Christian,* concludes: "Pilate, having symbolically washed his hands of the matter—the goofiest gesture, perhaps, of all time—gave the green light for judicial murder, directing that Jesus, though guiltless, should die all the same to keep people happy. Pilate saw this as shrewd government; how cynical can you get?"[4]

Pilate had the last clear chance to stop the charade. He had the power to call out the troops, quell the rioters, and send Jesus on his way. Instead, he went down in history as a weak and foolish man, his name intoned each week by hundreds of millions of Christians in the words of the Apostles' Creed: "I believe in God the Father almighty, maker of heaven and earth; and in Jesus Christ his only Son our Lord, who was conceived by the Holy Ghost, born of the Virgin Mary. Suffered under Pontius Pilate . . ."

It is interesting to note that both Pilate and Herod, who seemed to have been such thoroughly political humans, came to bad ends partly due to their own machinations. During their brief moment at the center stage of history, each had a clear choice—what to do with this Jesus of Nazareth?

chapter 9
THE PUNISHMENT

We know that Jesus of Nazareth died sometime between A.D. 30 and 33 (because of discrepancies in the early calendars we cannot be sure). He died in the spring. Before uttering his last words, whether they were "Father forgive them" or "Why have you forsaken me?" he suffered pain and anguish on the cross that cannot be expressed in the written word.

The cross has become the most prevalent symbol of Christianity. Sacred art has focused on it for two millennia. It stands out as a horrible reminder of the evil in humankind, for how could any civilized group of people force a fellow human being to die in such a calculatedly savage way? Even the Roman writer Cicero condemned crucifixion as "crudelissimum taeterrimumque supplicium"—a most cruel and disgusting punishment. In our own language, the word *excruciating* was derived from the word *crucifixion* as a way to describe the most horrible pain imaginable.

Today we may try to refine the jagged wooden cross into a beautiful gold-leaf ornament above our altars. Ministers tend not to dwell long on the grim details. But this alchemy of ours is not strong enough to hide its horror. We live in a time when cruelty is deplored. Our courts may sentence people to prison, but once there, the prisoners are provided with books, televisions, recreation, counseling, worship services, medical care, job training, rehabilitation, and much more. Our penal system is by no means an easy place to live—nor was it meant to be—but we no longer cut off the hands of thieves, burn out the tongues of' child abusers, or torture and decapitate rapists. We live in a relatively enlightened era, and our enlightenment is due, in large part, to a man named Jesus who taught a higher rule—a golden one.

But for that same Jesus the cross was wood, not gold. To understand the meaning of the trial we must understand the gruesome details of his punishment. A death sentence was not unusual in Jerusalem. But few men suffered the repeated humiliation and extreme pain that Jesus did.

A CATALOG OF JESUS' SUFFERING

After Jesus was arrested in Gethsemane, his hands were tied and he was forced to march to Annas's house. There he was slapped across the face for impudence. Hands still tied, he was taken to the Sanhedrin. There he was spat upon and ridiculed. Pilate ordered the Roman guard to flog Jesus. The whip had a dozen or more leather thongs, each with a piece of iron or bone tied to the end to tear the skin off the back and start deep bleeding. In Herod's court he was dressed in shabby rags of royal purple, a mock crown of thorns piercing his brow.

Already bruised and bleeding, he was displayed before a mob that screamed for his crucifixion. He carried his own heavy cross through the streets until, weakened by the loss of blood, he dropped from exhaustion. Finally arriving at Golgotha, he was nailed through the arms and feet to a wooden cross, which was then lifted upright and dropped with an excruciating jolt into a hole in the ground. As he hung there, limp and writhing, his muscles and ligaments tore away from his bones.

Jesus Christ's execution on the cross was gruesome and disgraceful, with extreme suffering, and was not the romantic death of some legends. A pathologist named Richter has summarized the medical evidence of the process of dying by crucifixion:

> . . . the unnatural position and violent tension of the body, which cause a painful sensation from the least movement . . . The nails, being driven through parts of the hands and feet which are full of nerves and tendons (and yet at a distance from the heart) create the most exquisite anguish. . . . The exposure of so many wounds and lacerations brings on inflammation, which tends to become gangrene, and every movement increases the poignancy of suffering. . . . In the distended parts of the body, more blood flows through the arteries than can be carried back into the veins: hence too much blood finds its way from the aorta into the head and stomach, and the blood vessels of the head become pressed and swollen. The general obstruction of circulation which ensues causes an intense excitement, exertion, and anxiety more intolerable than death itself. . . . The inexpressible misery of gradually increasing and lingering anguish. . . . Burning and raging thirst.[1]

Some men survived on the cross for many hours. After a few hours, in fact, the Roman soldiers were ordered to break the legs of the crucified, thereby increasing the weight on the arms and speeding the death of the victim. It was, in effect, a coup de grace, a way of limiting the extent of their agonies. When the soldiers came to break Jesus' legs, however, he was already dead (John 19:33).

So why did Jesus die in only a few hours? Part of the

explanation is found in the physical strength of the victim and in his physical position on the cross. But most likely, Jesus' death was hastened by the earlier floggings, writes Dr. William D. Edwards, a pathologist at the Mayo Clinic in Rochester, Minnesota. "There is perhaps not enough appreciation of what Christ suffered."[2] His analysis, co-written with a Methodist pastor and a medical illustrator, concludes that Jesus died from shock due to blood loss and because the weight of his body pulling down on his outstretched arms and shoulders made breathing difficult.

THE PRACTICE OF CRUCIFIXION

Recent archaeological finds in Israel have cast a new light on the crucifixion. Our standard artistic depiction of a cross may be incorrect. In 1968 in a cemetery at Gi'vat Ha-Mivtar, a bulldozer unearthed the skeletal remains of a young man named Yehohanan, or John. He was nailed to a T-shaped cross, his legs slung sideways in a crouched position. One nail penetrated the sides of his feet below the heel.

The skeleton was analyzed by Dr. Nico Haas of the Department of Anatomy at Hebrew University in Jerusalem. He concluded the man was "in a compulsive position, a difficult and unnatural posture."[3] This was done, apparently, to increase the agony. The torso was contorted and there was one iron nail in each forearm (not in the palms as is so often depicted in Christian art) so that the man's writhing caused the nails to scar the arm bones approximately two inches above the wrists. Of course, this man was not Jesus, so the details of the crucifixion may differ, but he was crucified in Jerusalem at approximately the same period and buried in a cave just outside the old city.

Other examples of death by crucifixion have been recorded; for instance, this one from an ancient Arabian manuscript:

A Victim of Crucifixion. A reconstructive sketch based on the remains of a crucified man unearthed at the cemetery at Gi'vat Ha-Mivtar in 1968. Note the position of the legs and the placement of the nails.

It is said that he killed his master for some cause or other, and he was crucified on the banks of the river Barada under the castle of Damascus, with his face turned toward the East. His hands, arms, and feet were nailed, and he remained so from midday on Friday to the same hour on Sunday, when he died. He was remarkable for his strength and prowess; he had been engaged with his master in sacred war at Askelon, where he slew great numbers of the Franks; and when very young he had killed a lion. Several extraordinary things occurred at his being nailed, as that he gave himself up without resistance to the cross, and without complaint stretched out his hands, which were nailed and after them his feet: he in the meantime looked on, and did not utter a groan, or change his countenance, or move his limbs. I have heard this from one who witnessed it, and he thus remained until he died, patient and silent, without wailing, but looking

around him to the right and left upon the people. But
he begged for water, and none was given him, and he
gazed upon it and longed for one drop of it, and he
complained of thirst all the first day, after which he
was silent, for God gave him strength.[4]

Crucifixion was still practiced in some parts of the world as
recently as the nineteenth century, as the Reverend Mr. Ellis
describes in an account of his experiences in Madagascar in
1875:

In a few cases of great enormity, a sort of crucifixion
has been resorted to; and, in addition to this, burning
or roasting at a slow fire, kept some distance from the
sufferer, has completed the horrors of this miserable
death . . . In the year 1825, a man was condemned to
crucifixion, who had murdered a female for the sake of
stealing her child. He carried the child for sale to the
public market, where the infant was recognized, and
the murderer detected. He bore his punishment in the
most hardened manner, avenging himself by all the
violence he was capable of exercising upon those who
dragged him to the place of execution. Not a single
groan escaped him during the period he was nailed to
the wood, nor while the cross was fixed upright in the
earth.[5]

In the time of Jesus, crucifixion was a Roman penalty, not a
Jewish one. It was so cruel that it was forbidden to crucify a
Roman citizen, except in certain cases of treason. Yet Pilate
had not found Jesus guilty of any crime against Caesar. Why
was Jesus not executed in the Jewish manner? Why were his
accusers not forced to corroborate the testimony of false
witnesses? Why were the accusers not required to inflict the
death penalty themselves?

CRUCIFIXION AND CHRIST'S ACCUSERS

The Jewish punishments for capital crimes were specific. Each was linked to a certain offense and served as an example to the populace. Since the Jews believed that capital punishment was a deterrent to crime, their punishments were brutal. Death was meted out in one of four ways: beheading, strangling, burning, and stoning. Murder was punished by lashing the criminal to a pole and beheading with a sword. Those guilty of false prophecy or one of five other crimes were given slower deaths. The criminal was buried to the waist and strangled with a cord in a soft cloth around the neck. Rape, incest, and eight other crimes were punished by placing the criminal in a pit, burying him up to the waist, and placing a lighted wick in his mouth. The flame slowly burned from inside out. Eighteen crimes, including blasphemy and magic, were punished by pushing the criminal off a cliff, and then stoning the still-breathing man to death.

According to the Sanhedrin, Jesus had committed blasphemy, though he was never punished for that crime. Some scholars believe that by A.D. 33 the Sanhedrin had lost the power of capital punishment. It is possible that the Romans had withdrawn this right from the Jews, for the Gospels indicate that the Sanhedrin needed Pilate to confirm the sentence. Yet once it was confirmed, why did the Jews want Jesus crucified instead of stoned?

One possible explanation is set out in the Talmud in a passage written two centuries after Christ. It states that "forty years before the destruction of the Temple the judgment of capital cases was taken away from Israel." The temple was destroyed in A.D. 70 when the Romans ruthlessly quashed a Zealot rebellion and leveled Jerusalem. If the Talmud is correct, then in A.D. 30, Pilate forbade the Jews to put a man to death, reserving that right for Rome. In this scenario, if the Jews wanted to execute Jesus, then Rome had to do it, and the Roman method of execution was crucifixion.

Another explanation is that the Jews wanted Jesus to die a Roman death to weaken his claim as the Messiah, for no Jew would believe the Messiah could die on a cross, or "tree." Deuteronomy 21:23 had already clearly stated that "anyone who is hung on a tree is under God's curse" (Deuteronomy 21:23). Furthermore, the Jews may have wanted his death to be an example to prevent widespread revolution. The Jewish authorities, already harshly oppressed by their Roman overlords, were eager to prevent any further suppression.

Finally, the Sanhedrin probably preferred a Roman execution simply as a way of frightening Christ's own followers. We can see from Peter's three denials that he was certainly frightened before the crucifixion. We can only imagine the fear Peter and his fellow disciples knew after watching their teacher die such a hideous death.

If Jesus had not reappeared on the road to Emmaus, the disciples would probably have remained too frightened to risk their lives (Luke 24:13–49). He showed them his hands and feet. They saw the wounds in his flesh-and-blood reappearance three days after his death. No wonder they were filled with awe and joy. As Paul would write later, "God forbid that I should boast of anything but the cross of our Lord Jesus Christ" (Galatians 6:14 NEB).

The hideousness of the death only highlights the gloriousness of the resurrection. Ultimately we are left with this question: What do we make of Jesus? A man who had suffered the kind of death he had would be unlikely to forgive his enemies or to tell the disciples to spread a message of hope and love throughout the world. Jesus was either the Son of God, heroically denying himself the right to call down legions of angels to save him—or else he was a madman of uncommon strength, carrying out a fraudulent bid for martyrdom without exposing a hint of the sham.

PART FOUR
The Modern Verdict

chapter 10

THE POLITICAL SHOW TRIAL

We live in an age of show trials. Among the most memorable in the past fifty years were Josef Stalin's purges of the 1930s. In these highly political dramas, Stalin sought to rid his government of traitors; anyone who was not personally loyal to him was in jeopardy. Thousands lost their lives, and many thousands more were sent to Siberia on the flimsiest of charges.

Aleksandr Solzhenitsyn described these trials in *The Gulag Archipelago*. In one passage, he tells of a special session of a local court that was held to make an example of certain defendants, Communists, and party officials who had fallen out of favor with Stalin. In such a crassly political confrontation, clearly neither justice nor truth played a role:

Though all the accused declined defense lawyers, a government lawyer was forced on them so that the case wouldn't be left without a prosecutor. The formal indictment, solemn, menacing, and lengthy, came down in essence to the charge that an underground Rightist Bukharinite group has existed in the Kady District . . . and had as its purpose the overthrow by

147

wrecking of the Soviet government in the village of Kady (and this was about the remotest boondock in all Russia the rightists could have found for a starting point!).

The prosecutor petitioned the court to have Stavrov's testimony, given before his death in prison, read to the court and accepted as evidence. In fact, the whole charge against the group was based on Stavrov's evidence. The court agreed to include the testimony of the deceased, just as if he were alive. (With advantage, however, that none of the defendants could refute it.)

The testimony of Stavrov, who had been killed under interrogation, was read to the Court and once again became part of the record. The questioning of the defendants began—and immediately there was chaos. All of them repudiated the testimony they had given during the interrogation.

The judge rebuked the defendants: How could you have given different testimony during the interrogation? Univer, very weak, replied in a barely audible voice: "As a Communist I cannot, in a public trial describe the interrogation methods of the NKVD [The secret police]."[1]

Univer meant, of course, that under torture they had admitted to fictional crimes. Even dead men like Stavrov were allowed to testify from the grave by affidavits obtained under torture. There was no right to confront and cross-examine witnesses, no right against self-incrimination. The phony trials were a tool to punish the people outside the mainstream of Communist party ideology.

These trials were never intended to determine truth and then do justice; they were shams to achieve a political end that those in power believed was far more important than the individual lives involved. The ends were so important to the Stalinists that even the most outrageous means were rationalized. A wave of political show trials engulfed the communist world. Victor Serge, another brilliant observer of these events and a reformed Communist, described them in *Memoirs of a Revolutionary*:

> The most shameless lying conceivable blazed out before our very eyes. But as witnesses we were practically gagged. In *Pravda* I could read the accounts (all of them mangled) of the Trials. I picked out literally hundreds of improbabilities, absurdities, gross distortions of fact, utterly lunatic statements. But it was a deluge of delirium. Scarcely had I analyzed one billow of flagrant deceit than another, more violent, would wash away my day's work into futility. The torrent was so overwhelming that one could never find one's bearings.[2]

In more recent times the Ayatollah Kohmeini attempted to put American hostages on trial for espionage. His twin motives were to humiliate America and to temper his own political power base through the Iranian student organizations and the Mullahs. President Carter passed a message to Kohmeini through diplomatic channels that if any hostages were put on trial, America would intervene. President Carter understood the power and significance of a political show trial and, in this case, was able to prevent one.

The political show trial is frequently used in South Africa and other countries that are struggling with the unrest caused by racial and economic injustice. In our own country, the early 1950s brought us the political spy trials of the Rosenbergs, together with Senator McCarthy's Un-American Activities hearings. This practice of putting a political adversary on trial has gone on, nonstop, since that time. Many of us can still remember the Francis Gary Powers spy trial in Moscow; the Angela Davis trial; and the trials of the Chicago Seven.

Authorities stage show trials to sway public opinion. They use them to make loud and clear political statements about their own ideological standards and to undermine their enemies at the same time. Show trials are philosophic in nature, and in many cases, justice and truth take a backseat to ideological concerns, and above all, the message in most show trials is more important than the fate of any one person.

But the denial of justice is not always the case, however. Not all show trials are shams; some can be used potently for good. After World War II, for instance, many Nazi officials were tried for war crimes in the highly publicized Nuremberg Trials. The civilized world had thwarted a great evil by defeating the Nazis and ending the Holocaust. When the fighting was over, the legal system helped evaluate the guilt of individuals and impose punishment. Although the point of these trials was clearly ideological, they spread the message throughout the world that crimes against humanity would not be tolerated.

It was not nearly so important to send Albert Speer to prison as to show the world that he, as Hitler's architect and Nazi planning minister, must be held accountable for his actions. Men have free will to choose between good and evil. The show trial can be an honest search for truth. The challenge to the observer is to distinguish between the serious and the sham, the principle and the phony.

Another example of a political show trial that resulted in good is the John Goldmark libel trial in Okanogan County, Washington. It helped to vindicate a man who had been the victim of some of the worst in small-town demagoguery. John Goldmark was a Harvard-educated lawyer, a decorated World War II veteran, and a leading Democratic state legislator in Washington. Some members of the local John Birch Society, who despised Goldmark's liberal views, branded him a Communist. Though he was not, the stigma caused him to lose his election. The anti-communists' strategy had worked. Goldmark had been falsely labeled and vilified in the press and at public meetings, and his career had been ruined. Goldmark had no choice but to sue.

As Bill Dwyer, Goldmark's lawyer, later described it in his book *The Goldmark Case,* the primary objective was to convince the jurors that reputation is at the heart of our existence, that the law of libel was not a matter of legal technicalities. His hope was that they would recognize that the power of the written and spoken word is the power of life and death over a man's existence.

"A man's good name has been attacked," wrote Dwyer, "destroyed, vilified, dragged through the mud, not once, not twice, but practically every day for a period that is now going on to be two years. . . . It is no exaggeration to say that life without a good name is hardly worth living. He has to fight for his good name, not only for his sake but for the sake of his family. . . . The Ninth Commandment in the Bible is that 'Thou shalt not bear false witness against thy neighbor.' "[3]

Dwyer proceeded to describe to the jury the libels spread by the defendants, which were of the worst type. "A man who is called a communist is called a traitor to his country, an enemy to his country." One so condemned would be followed everywhere by a cloud of ill will and suspicion; nor would his children escape it. "These are the reasons that this case had to be tried here in Okanogan County and not in Seattle and not in Spokane and not anywhere else. Because it is here that the Goldmarks' reputation is for good or bad. This is their home."[4]

Bill Dwyer, now a federal judge in Seattle, successfully convinced the jury that Goldmark had been libeled. As a result, his name is now held up in honor and respect among most people in that community.

The Berrigan brothers went on trial in the early 1970s for their anti-war protests, and since that time there have been hundreds of political trials in the United States. The trials have concerned every imaginable issue from the Trident

Nuclear Submarine Base at Bangor, Washington, to the Clamshell Alliance protestors on the coast of Maine. Anti-apartheid protestors are arrested daily in South Africa for their confrontational behavior. People all over the world are being imprisoned and fined for their political views. Of course, in America the key issue is whether they are taking their political opinions out of the protected area of free speech, and into the realm of violence and action contrary to the law. We have the right to cry out any crackpot idea on the street corner, but not to yell "Fire!" in a crowded theater.

Thomas F. O'Meara, professor of Systematic Theology at Aquinas Institute, has noted another theme in political show trials. He believes that one unifying feature is that the defendants switch roles with the prosecutors. In a truly political trial the defendant becomes the accuser, in a sense, and the accusers become the accused.[5]

The risks that prosecutors take in initiating a show trial is that of allowing the accused to state his or her own views. Instead of defeating the political enemy, the degradation of the accused becomes a statement that can actually turn public opinion against the accusers. Exactly the opposite of what the authorities had planned. In most show trials, the best defense an accused person can present is to try to perform such a reversal. When this happens, the results are memorable.

The most famous recent example of an attempted reversal was Oliver North's aggressive patriotic stance at the Congressional hearings over the Iran-Contra weapons-for-hostages swap. Senator Inoye began the hearings and was stern and antagonistic toward Admiral Poindexter and Robert McFarland. But Lt. Col. North "wrapped himself in the flag," accused Congress of being a source of leaks, and implied that if Congress had not been so weak, America would yet be strong. For many North became an instant folk hero by brilliantly turning the tables on the committee that was examining him.

In the trial that followed, the prosecutor spent millions of dollars to get a conviction on relatively minor charges. Was it worthwhile? Even so, the verdict was appealed, in spite of North's light sentence. But the issues at stake were significant to Americans: the separation of powers among the branches of government and the direction of foreign policy in Central America and the Middle East.

North may have been a highly decorated military hero, a brave and honorable man only doing his duty, but as a decision maker at the nexus of power he had certain responsibilities. He had to make choices, such as whether to lie to Congress to cover up what he thought to be a greater good. Though no doubt sincere, he made choices that put him in the center of a political controversy that guaranteed his trial would be the show trial of the eighties. The issues were what were on trial. Congressmen could not tolerate a witness who intentionally misled them, and they appropriated money for special counsel Walsh to make an example of North and regain the power in the constant struggle between the legislative and executive branches of government.

In the twentieth century we have such a wide-ranging experience in the strategies of these kinds of political trial, and such extensive scholarship on the trial of Jesus, that we are in a unique position to appreciate the lessons of that trial 2000 years ago. Jesus was caught in a power struggle between the priests and the Romans. His choices, actions, preaching, miracles, and Sabbath-breaking guaranteed that his trial would be the show trial of all time.

THE POLITICAL SHOW TRIAL OF JESUS

Every culture defines its own taboos and its own boundaries on free speech. According to the rabbis then in power, Jesus of Nazareth had crossed that line. He had tipped over the tables in the temple. He had prophesied he would destroy

and then rebuild the temple in three days. He caused the
people to grow unruly. He had to be stopped.

In the tradition of later political show trials, Jesus was
labeled by his enemies and framed for ideological reasons.
The trial was intended to publicly disgrace Jesus and his
followers, and crush his new religious teachings. His trial was
one of the first great show trials in history, and it has had
more significance for the entire world than any trial since.

But by claiming to be both God and man, he was, in a
sense, too much for any one legal system to handle. So after
being accused of both religious and political crimes, he was
tried in the legal systems of two cultures—by God's chosen
people, the Jews, as well as by the Gentiles. The religious
crime of which he was accused was that of stating he was the
Son of God, which for the Jews was the height of blasphemy,
and the political crime was that of causing people to riot—
insurrection. After being charged, he was brought to trial
twice; once before the highest religious body in the land, the
Sanhedrin, and then a second time before the all-powerful
political force of Judea, the Roman governor, Pilate. He was
even examined by the hated King Herod, though whether that
interview constituted a trial is open to question.

These two trials were significant, for had Jesus been tried
only as a Jew in front of the Sanhedrin, the historian Josephus
most likely would never have mentioned him, and it is also
likely that the gentile world would have heard much less of
the man and his teachings. Had he been tried only by the
Romans as a political rebel, he would not have had the forum
for proclaiming that he was the Messiah, the Son of God.
Jesus said he was the bridge between God and man, and the
unique two-trial format allowed him to be just that, for both
the chosen people and the Gentiles.

The dual nature of this trial distinguishes it from Socrates'
earlier trial in Athens. While Socrates was charged with
blaspheming the Olympian gods and attempting to destroy the

Pilate Showing Christ to the People. Woodcut by Albrecht Dürer from his "Great Passion" illustrations, 1510. Note that even the child in the left foreground holds a stick, with which, presumably, he will beat the condemned man.

constitution of the Attic Republic, he was a great philosopher who never claimed to be a god or a "Son of Man." His was a purely political trial. Socrates was accused of leading astray the youth of Athens by his anti-democratic teaching. The established political power was pro-democracy and saw Socrates as a dangerous influence, and the religious charges were trumped up to sway public opinion against him. The teacher had used his freedom of speech to directly challenge the status quo. The recent book by I. F. Stone, *The Trial of Socrates,* is a wonderful examination of this Athenian political show trial. Although great issues were at stake in the trial of Socrates—academic freedom, democracy versus dictatorship—the issues in the trial of Jesus were more than merely political. They were deeply religious as well.

Not only was Jesus accused and labeled by his accusers, but typical of many victims of show trials, he was successfully able to perform a role reversal, to turn the tables on his accusers. Though condemned to die, he was able to transcend the limitations of the legal system and teach lessons to the world that would become eternal. When Christ stepped peacefully into the courtroom, he knew that it was his opportunity to take the stand and show the world his love for and obedience to his Father. He did not cower and avoid the confrontation. By example he led his disciples forward. And this example became a subtle accuser of those who had accused him.

The trial itself, ultimately, was an integral part of his message, the essence being that he was born both God and man, that he was killed, and that his death washed away our sins. By dying for mankind, he took away the sting of death. To make all these implicit statements, Christ had to be killed in this profound and public way, judged by two societies—his own people and by the most powerful nation in the world.

The trials themselves are lessons in human injustice, since we have to ask what kind of legal system could crucify the symbol of God's love in a human body? From a lawyer's viewpoint, the very thought that our system is capable of such a gross injustice is a sign of the dark side of man.

But the truth of this message goes beyond man's injustice; it hinges on the divine nature of Jesus. He must be the link not only between the religious and political cultures of the time, but also between the earth and heaven. His role as the Son of God and Savior of mankind is what allowed his message to transcend his trial and death. By his resurrection Jesus performs a kind of role reversal with the final judge— death. Ultimately, that is the source of his message's authority and the root of the universality of his sacrifice and hope for the earth.

Christ's unique role as the Son of God is the framework for this entire study. In *Mere Christianity,* C. S. Lewis states that if Christ were not divine, then his message was pointless:

> I am trying here to prevent anyone saying the really foolish thing that people often say about Him: "I am ready to accept Jesus as a great moral teacher, but I don't accept His claim to be God." That is the one thing we must not say. A man who is merely a man and said the sort of things Jesus said would not be a great moral teacher. He would either be a lunatic—on a level with the man who says he is a poached egg—or else he would be the Devil of Hell. You must make your choice. Either this man was, and is, the Son of God; or else a madman, or something worse. You can shut Him up for a fool, you can spit at Him and kill Him as a demon, or you can fall at His feet and call Him Lord and God. Let us not come with any patronizing nonsense about His being a great human teacher. He has not left that open to us. He did not intend to.[6]

But the message of the hope for salvation that arises from Christ's trial, death, and resurrection is not always clear to us. We are, all of us, ignorant about spiritual things. While it only takes a moment to give your heart to Jesus, it takes years to learn many of the fine points of his message. This was true for the early disciples as well. In John 14:21–23, after Jesus has described to his disciples how he would show himself after his death, Judas (not Judas Iscariot) asks a question that, by that time in Jesus' ministry, seems a bit naive: "But, Lord, why do you intend to show yourself to us and not to the world?"

The point that Judas is missing is that he still expects Jesus to fulfill the popular messianic notions of a warrior king who would violently overthrow the Romans and establish a new kingdom in Jerusalem. When Jesus said that he would reveal himself to the disciples only, it must have been a disappointment. Even though Jesus had already explained that he would do something even greater, many of the disciples still did not understand.

Surely if this scene were fictional, the author would have given Judas a more perceptive question. The very ignorance underlying the question is more evidence that the Gospels are an authentic reproduction of what the author saw and heard, rather than what he would have chosen to say.

As maturing Christians, what do we make of a disciple going off in the wrong direction? Jesus tells us. He uses Judas's question as a springboard for an exciting revelation:

> All this I have spoken while still with you. But the Counselor, the Holy Spirit, whom the Father will send in my name, will teach you all things and will remind you of everything I have said to you. Peace I leave with you; my peace I give you. I do not give to you as the world gives. Do not let your hearts be troubled and do not be afraid.
>
> You heard me say, "I am going away and I am coming back to you." If you loved me, you would be glad that I am going to the Father, for the Father is

greater than I. I have told you now before it happens,
so that when it does happen you will believe. (John
14:25–29)

Jesus is teaching the disciples the meaning behind his trial
and death. He not only introduces the Holy Spirit who will
take his place, but he answers our question, "Why a trial?"
In John 14:30–31, he states: "I will not speak with you much
longer, for the prince of this world is coming. He has no hold
on me, but the world must learn that I love the Father and
that I do exactly what my Father has commanded me." In
other words, his obedience to God is primary, and because of
his obedience, death cannot bind him. That is the greatest
reversal of all time.

chapter 11
CIVIL DISOBEDIENCE

According to the Gospels, the Sanhedrin, not having the power to put a criminal to death, accused Jesus of sedition—that is, plotting the violent overthrow of the Roman government in Judea—so that the Romans would be forced to execute him. The charge was trumped up. The Sanhedrin was attempting to frame him.

JESUS AS A ZEALOT

That Jesus was in fact a Zealot, however, has been strenuously insisted upon by S. G. F. Brandon, a professor at the University of Manchester, England. Brandon's theory is a variant of the modern Jewish approach to the trial—that Jesus was a political revolutionary and died as a convicted enemy of Rome. Brandon admits that the Gospel accounts of the trial "have preserved the only detailed evidence we have of it," but he assumes that the three later Gospels, Matthew, Luke, and John, are all based on Mark's Gospel and are therefore essentially hearsay.[1]

In Brandon's view, the Romans crucified Jesus on a cross,

an ignominious death after which the early Christians wanted to place the blame on the Jews. Brandon argues that they created a story that made Christ an innocent martyr. According to Brandon, therefore, the Gospels are nothing more than an apologetic, Christian propaganda written because the church was embarrassed that their God had been crucified as a common criminal. Brandon ends his criticism of the Gospels with these words:

> None of them [Matthew, Luke, and John] substantially differs from the major theme of Mark's presentation. For, like him, they seek to show that the Jews were responsible for the crucifixion of Jesus and that they show a similar reluctance to disclose the nature of the charges which the Jews brought against Jesus, and on which Pilate condemned him. Their accounts are no more careful records of a trial than is Mark's; for they follow him in describing what is really a contest between Pilate and the Jews over the fate of Jesus. Similarly, the contradictions, absurdities, reticence and elusiveness manifest in these accounts are all found to stem from the embarrassing fact of the Roman execution of Jesus for sedition. Although in certain ways their motives differed from that which produced Mark's apologetic version of the trial, Matthew, Luke and John shared his concern to make Pilate a witness to the innocence of Jesus, and the Jews solely responsible for his death.[2]

Brandon's basic assumptions are:

—The Romans executed Jesus for sedition.
—Pilate believed Jesus guilty of the crime.
—Jesus was, in fact, guilty of sedition.
—Jesus came to Jerusalem to accomplish a messianic coup d'état aimed primarily at the priestly aristocracy.
—Jesus foresaw the likelihood of his own death by the

Roman method of crucifixion as a result of this open
rebellion.
—Jesus was crucified with two Zealots as a warning to
the Jews not to revolt against Rome.
—Jesus was a Zealot.

Are these assumptions based on fact? Are they logical?
These are significant questions for modern Christians. The
question, Was Jesus a Zealot? is relevant to our faith today.

If Jesus was a revolutionary, not only turning over tables
in the temple, but actively conspiring to overthrow the
Romans, then he associated with both murderers and patri-
ots. If Brandon's Jesus had been alive in 1944 he would have
advocated assassinating Hitler, as did Lutheran theologian
Dietrich Bonhoeffer. Were such a Zealot alive today he might
bomb government buildings in South Africa. According to
Brandon this Jesus was a firebrand who sought the new
kingdom in the politics of this world and not in some other
future time. This is very different from the pacifistic Jesus
that many Christians have aspired to follow.

Many Christians worship Brandon's revolutionary
Christ. For instance, an entire new school of action-oriented
priests in Latin America advocates "liberation theology." In
Nicaragua a Catholic priest joined the communist Sandinista
government. After being ordered by the Pope resume his
priestly duties, he defied the order and led an Easter Mass
parade, carrying both a crucifix and a Sandinista banner.
Government propaganda tries to draft Jesus into the Marxist
revolution. One book cover shows a crucified Christ and a
Soviet submachine-gun-toting guerrilla. The message is clear.
It asserts a direct link between Christ's sacrificial death and
the call for new martyrs for this modern revolution. Its title is
Christian Faith and the Sandinista Revolution.

Many scholars, of course, disagree with Brandon. Professor D. R. Catchpole sets forth a compelling argument that
Christ was not a Zealot. Catchpole concludes that Brandon

Christian Faith and the Sandinista Revolution. Contemporary book cover from Nicaragua.

ignores evidence that doesn't fit his theories, makes assumptions, and exaggerates. If Jesus had been a Zealot, the soldiers would have arrested all of his followers as well. That they arrested only Christ and let the others go, even allowing some of them to follow Christ and witness the trial, indicates that they were not suspected of breaking the law.[3]

Malcolm Muggeridge, the well-known modern author, asserts that, "He scrupulously refrained from getting mixed up in Jewish nationalism, which was very strong . . . in Galilee, and He showed no disposition to resent his position as a member of a subject people."[4]

Also, Josephus in his *Antiquities of the Jews* devotes many pages to the Zealots and others who periodically led armed revolts against the Romans.[5] Nowhere in ancient Jewish history is Jesus cited as a Zealot by the Jews. Simply put, there is no primary ancient source that suggests Jesus was a Zealot.

JESUS AND CIVIL DISOBEDIENCE

Does this mean, however, that Jesus was against political involvement? How could a man's rights be so grossly violated without more of a protest from the victim himself? Should we, like him, willingly submit to the sometimes cruel and unjust decisions that a government makes? If we accept our chief evidence, which clearly shows Jesus was subjected to two unfair and illegal trials, does it seem credible for him to have submitted to the verdicts without complaint?

The answer to these questions is: It depends. That is, it depends upon whether the government has a legitimate right to expect and enforce such obedience. Most nations have established, by both written laws and customs, the areas subject to governmental control. For example, the power to arrest and imprison criminals is almost universally acknowledged a function of government, as is the power to impose and collect taxes. The power to schedule a holiday on a given date is a right accorded to the government, but the power to observe the events symbolized by that holiday is one that an individual either exercises or ignores.

A frequently quoted verse on this subject begins with the phrase "Render unto Caesar that which is Caesar's." The teaching has been often discussed by preachers and dissected by scholars. Its meaning is important to modern Christians.

Several times in the last hundred years, serious Christians have faced the problem of whether to take up arms and kill other human beings or to be conscientious objectors. This chapter will not tackle that problem. We will, however, explore the dilemma posed by the trial of Jesus of living "in the world" but not being "of the world," of how we follow the steps of Jesus without contributing to the unrighteousness of evil people. This spiritual "split personality" is not a new problem for the believer. A brief look at the history of Christianity and its attitude toward political and religious authority will be helpful.

The Roman historian Tertullian wrote in the first century that the Christians would not serve in the armed forces of Rome. He advised them to desert. Historian Edward Gibbon (1737–94) records that the Christians could not serve in the military or even in the political system without by so doing renouncing a more sacred duty. According to Gibbon, non-Christians viewed this as cowardly behavior:

> This indolent or even criminal disregard to the public welfare exposed them to the contempt and reproaches of the pagans, who very frequently asked, "What must be the fate of the empire, attacked on every side by the barbarians, if all mankind should adopt the pusillanimous sentiments of the new sect?" To this insulting question the Christian apologists returned obscure and ambiguous answers, as they were unwilling to reveal the secret cause of their security—the expectation that before the conversion of mankind was accomplished war, government, the Roman empire, and the world itself would be no more.[6]

As the years passed, the Christians lived through both passive and active persecution. The greatest persecutions took place during the rule of Emperor Diocletian. Although his wife and daughter were greatly attracted to Christianity, and the four principal eunuchs of the palace were converted, Diocletian ended eighteen years of religious toleration and deprived Christians of the protection of the law. His edicts led to the burning of churches, confiscation of all church property, and torture of Christians.

The church grew despite and perhaps because of the persecutions. In A.D. 324, a new age dawned. The Roman Emperor Constantine decreed that henceforth Christianity would be the official state religion. He was converted, although some scholars and modern politicians view his "rebirth" with skepticism. The church was no longer merely rendering unto Caesar; it belonged to Caesar. Though the persecution ended, the many healthy benefits of separation of church and state were lost, and inevitably, as power was centralized, the church as an institution became more corrupt. The authority of the government merged with the authority of the church.

Throughout the next millennium, the church grew and prospered both in souls and in gold. The great Gothic cathedrals were built by illiterate peasants. The church fathers themselves, often illiterate and immoral, were too frequently the blind leading the blind. The response among spiritual men and women was to discredit the existing religious establishment and call for a return to piety.

In the French villages of Languedoc around the year 1200, many common folk known as Cathars began an evolution into heresy in an attempt to seek a holier life than that offered by the profligate priests. The church mercilessly repressed the sect, which went underground to avoid persecution. Between 1300 and 1326 an official inquisition was made among the residents of Montaillou. Although the show trial was theological, there were serious political ramifications. The records of the examinations have been retained and were recently analyzed by LeRoy Ladurie in a fascinating book—*Montaillou—Promised Land of Error*:

> Devotion to the Apostles developed in the West after the eleventh century, linked to the discovery of the "apostolic life" and gradually being incorporated "into the realm of popular devotion." Pierre Maury was told by his co-parishioners (iii.120): "The good people and good Christians came into this country; they follow the path followed by the blessed Peter and Paul and the other Apostles, who followed the Lord . . . We ask you: would you like to meet the good Christians?"

> Pierre answered: "If the good men are as you say, if they do follow the path of the Apostles, why do they not preach publicly, as the Apostles did? . . . Why are they afraid for truth and justice, when the Apostles themselves were not afraid to suffer death for such a cause?"[7]

Why were these spiritual men and women afraid to publicly proclaim their faith? In the Middle Ages, men were members of a corporate body; either a village, town, or commune. Individuals rarely had the freedom to act outside the strict confines established by the church and society. These two governors of all men's lives were static and slow to change. The corruption of the church led to disillusionment among both the educated and the masses. For a detailed examination of this tumultuous period see *A Distant Mirror: The Calamitous Fourteenth Century* by Barbara Tuchman. As the official court transcript records the testimony:

> Belibaste to the Maurys of Montaillou (ii.25,26,56): "The Pope devours the blood and sweat of the poor. And the bishops and the priests, who are rich and honored and self-indulgent, behave in the same manner . . . whereas Saint Peter abandoned his wife, his children, his fields, his vineyards and his possessions to follow Christ." Belibaste rounded off his diatribe with the usual references to the clergy's sexual depravity (ii.26): "The bishops, the priests and the Minorite and preaching friars go to the houses of rich, young and beautiful women; they take their money and, if they consent, they sleep carnally with them, putting on appearances of humility the while." The parfaits contrasted the Church which fleeces with that which forgives (iii.123). Against the pomp of Rome, Belibaste set a minimal organization of a non-militant Church of God; the material Church is nothing.

These ideas found echoes in the villagers of
Montaillou and their friends the migrant shepherds.
Pierre Maury, for instance, vented his feelings on the
subject (i.29–30): The Minorite and preaching friars?
No! They call themselves little or "minor" and they
are big. Instead of saving the souls of the dead and
sending them to heaven, they gorge themselves at
banquets after funerals. And then they own too many
silks. And do you think that their great houses were
built by the labor of their own hands? No, these friars,
they are wicked wolves! They would like to devour us
all, dead or alive.[8]

The very church was caught in a papal schism when the
papacy at Rome was challenged by a usurper at the French
city of Avignon. Now two popes fought over who had
legitimate claim to Peter's line. The stage was set for the
Reformation. Once again spiritual individuals struggled to be
in the world but not of it. The materialistic, powerful church
had become so corrupt that change was inevitable.

John Wycliffe, a little-known Bible translator in England
in 1379, was convinced that both popes were corrupt. His
conclusion was that the only way to prevent the abuses then
rampant in Europe was to bring the church under secular
control. Since he believed that the King of England was
placed in that exalted position by God, he reasoned that the
divine right of kings included supervising the kingdom of God
on earth. Wycliffe was prepared to take his religious rebellion
to the people by way of his new translation of the Bible.
Although patronized by several wealthy Britons, he eventually frightened them with his reformist ardor. In 1381 twelve
professors at Oxford judged Wycliffe's ideas unorthodox and
heretical, and he was forbidden to lecture or preach. Yet he
and his followers continued their monumental task of trans-
lating the Scriptures, some 750,000 words, from Latin into
English. His work allowed the literate to learn directly about

God and the teachings of Christ, making the priestly middle-
men unnecessary. The readers could reason, worship, and
pray on their own. Wycliffe took the power of salvation from
the control of the corrupt church and gave it to Everyman. As
Barbara Tuchman observed: "Unperceived, here was the
start of the modern world."[9]

One of Wycliffe's tenets was that the bread and wine of
Communion do not actually become the body and blood of
Christ. Followed by Hus, Luther, and Calvin, he exposed the
foibles of priests: "How can the virtue of the sacrament be
communicated by an evil priest?" In this new world where
men could deny the role of priests it was only a matter of time
until men questioned the omnipotence of God.

Roland Bainton, the historian from Yale, applied his
scholarship to this critical period in *The Reformation of the
Sixteenth Century*. Luther argued that Christians needed to
"return to the simplicity of the New Testament, the scorn of
scholastic subtlety, the invective against indulgences, against
the veneration of relics, and against the cult of the saints." In
1520, in his *Babylonian Captivity,* Luther made public his
intellectual break with the Roman Catholic Church. Pope Leo
issued a Bull summoning Luther to explain himself within
sixty days or risk excommunication. Luther answered sixty
days later, on December 10, 1520, by publicly burning the
Bull and the Canon Law.[10]

Yet the fire that burned within such men as Wycliffe and
Luther failed to kindle the spirits of a majority of Christians.
Some pietists sought a spiritual purity and were willing to risk
social ostracism and even death to lead others to a new life,
but not all good spiritual men were willing to follow.
Desiderius Erasmus (1466–1536), a priest-philosopher, read
The Babylonian Captivity and exclaimed, "The breach is
irreparable!" Though He was unwilling to leave the church,
even with its flaws, he too was criticized by his fellow
churchmen as a free thinker; his writings, including the

famous "Colloquies," were denounced in 1526 by the faculty
of the University of Paris. The scholars believed the "Colloquies" corrupted the morals of the youth.

Erasmus, amid much suspicion, wanted to reform the
church from within. He disagreed with Luther about free will.
In 1524 Erasmus declared that man is capable of doing good
and evil, to which Luther answered that man's destiny lies
wholly in the hands of God, salvation being offered only to
those who have the gift of faith. Luther attributed the
acceptance of some and rejection of others to God's immuta-
ble decree. Erasmus asked why human anomalies should be
thus projected into eternity, and he preferred to leave man
insecure rather than incriminate God. Luther answered,
"God must be God."

The question of our freedom to choose good and evil is
an essential element of the struggle between reformer and
revisionist. It relates to the trial of Jesus (did Pilate have a
choice?) and to the basic problem of what we "render unto
Caesar." How free are we in dealing with the ultimate
problems of life? Luther stressed our duty to obey government. The religious establishment fought Luther much as the
ancient Jews sought to label Christ a Zealot and a subversive.
The only time a Christian can and should disobey his
government is when a ordinance is contrary to Christian
doctrine. A thoughtful discussion of this problem can be
found in Senator Mark Hatfield's *Between a Rock and a Hard
Place*.

The most common dilemma is whether to participate in
an unjust war, but a second popular issue is whether to
support nuclear weapons with tax money. Although normally
the government is the best judge of the "justness" of a war,
or the need for a weapons system, if a Christian in good
conscience believes himself in a position to evaluate the
justness and concludes the war or weapon to be immoral,
then must he not, as a Christian, refuse to support the

immorality? The issue of abortion is another example. The courts have ruled abortion is legal, but is it moral?

The point is that Christians have a long history of having their ideas tried before religious and civil courts, and before the court of public opinion. These courts are sometimes sympathetic, sometimes hostile. Ultimately, however, obedience to God and a willingness to speak the truth are the only sure defense. They are the best means of being in the world, to change it for the better, but not being of it.

But we must choose. Can we ignore the moral imperatives of our age, or do we risk our reputations, our comfort, our financial well-being by going on trial before the governments and judges of this world, as Jesus did in his time? A Christian should understand his dual role as a citizen of this world and a citizen of the kingdom of God. He needs to follow Christ's example of submitting to the jurisdiction of both courts—while knowing that, ultimately, whatever the cost, he must obey his God.

Our image of a submissive Christ, however, is no more accurate than the image of a guerrilla Christ. Jesus did indeed challenge the authorities. When he stood before Annas, he did not meekly submit to the inquisition. He spoke the truth boldly, and for this he was struck on the face. Later, before the Sanhedrin and knowing the trial was a mockery of justice, he refused to play into the hands of the powerful priests. He answered their questions at times, and remained silent at other times.

Pilate was interested in Jesus as a curiosity, a rare person, a wise and spiritual man who was despised by his own people. Jesus could have called off the charade. At one point he told Pilate, "You would have no power over me if it were not given to you by my Father in heaven." Yet he did not call for a host of angels to carry him out of the courtroom, nor did he make the Roman standards bow. Rather, Jesus submitted his will to God. He allowed himself to be mocked, scourged, beaten, bloodied, humiliated, and crucified. His example is the standard for Christians who want to be in this world but not of it.

Albert Schweitzer, the brilliant, multifaceted man who, among many outstanding achievements, wrote *The Quest for the Historical Jesus,* concluded that book with these words:

> He comes to us as One unknown, without a name, as of old by the lake-side, He came to those men who knew Him not. He speaks to us the same word: "Follow thou me!" and sets us to the tasks which He has to fulfil for our time. He commands. And to those who obey Him, whether they be wise or simple, He will reveal himself in the toils, the conflicts, the sufferings, which they shall pass through in His fellowship, and, as an ineffable mystery, they shall learn in their own experience Who He is.[11]

Truth and obedience, then, are the greatest weapons a believer has, whether that believer be a Zealot or a pacifist, a liberal or a conservative. Speaking the truth and obeying God are the primary lessons we can learn from Jesus' participation in his trials. We have the freedom to choose whether we will serve God in these ways. If we choose the weapons of truth and obedience, we may be imprisoned, disgraced, or even put to death; but ultimately all the armies and protests and governments of the world cannot withstand their power.

chapter 12

THE CLOSING ARGUMENT

All the evidence is now before the court. It is time for the attorneys to marshal the facts in compelling closing arguments. The skeptic will point to the inconsistencies in the Gospel accounts and the foolish exaggerations in the Apocrypha and the Jewish and Moslem versions. The Christian lawyer can point to the many consistencies of the Gospels, the marvelous accuracies confirmed by the Dead Sea Scrolls and ancient rock carvings.

The judge and jury must decide the case by evaluating the facts and then applying the law to those facts. A typical jury instruction, given at the conclusion of the presentation of evidence, reads as follows:

> You are the sole judges of credibility of the witnesses and of what weight is to be given the testimony of each. In considering the testimony of any witness, you may take into account the opportunity and ability of the witness to observe, the witness's memory and manner while testifying, any interest, bias, or prejudice the witness may have, the reasonableness of the testimony of the witness considered in light of all the

evidence, and any other factors that bear on believabil-
ity and weight.[1]

I hope I have convinced you that the evidence of the
Gospel writers is believable, falling well within the legally
accepted test set forth by Professor Starkie in the nineteenth
century, and also within the modern guidelines of the Federal
Rules of Evidence. Scientific research and historical investi-
gation have not disproven the Gospels; in fact, they have
confirmed their claims.

Look carefully at the opinions of the experts. C. F. D.
Moule concludes:

> It is difficult enough for anyone, even a consummate
> master of imaginative writing, to create a picture of a
> deeply pure, good person moving about in an impure
> environment, without making him a prig or a prude or a
> sort of plaster saint.
>
> How comes it that, through all the Gospel tradi-
> tions without exception, there comes a remarkably
> firmly drawn portrait of an attractive young man
> moving freely about among women of all sorts,
> including the decidedly disreputable, without a trace of
> sentimentality, unnaturalness, or prudery, and yet, at
> every point, maintaining a simple integrity of char-
> acter?
>
> Is this because the environments in which the
> traditions were preserved and through which they were
> transmitted were particularly favorable to such a
> portrait? On the contrary, it seems that they were
> hostile to it.[2]

T. W. Manson concludes: "I am increasingly convinced
that in the Gospels we have the materials—reliable materials—for an outline account of the ministry as a whole."[3]

John Knox concludes: "[The Gospels leave us] with a

very substantial residuum of historically trustworthy facts about Jesus, his teachings and his life."[4]

Historian Michael Grant concludes: "The consistency, therefore, of the tradition in their pages suggests that the picture they present is largely authentic."[5]

Just as these experts testify to the reliability of the Gospels, thousands of historical documents and the very stones of the early Christian churches themselves cry out that Jesus lived. Although the entire known world has been transformed by learning and technology in these past 2000 years, the message of Jesus remains unchanged. The evidence is conclusive: Jesus lived and died to bring that message to humanity.

All the evidence is now before the court: hundreds of documents, mountains of stone and artifacts, miles of parchments, papyrus, and propaganda. The Apocrypha, the histories, the evidence of the Roman and the Jewish writers, all of these now have been brought before the judge and jury. The expert witnesses have testified, from Brandon to Catchpole, hundreds of scholars, with their thousands of pages of treatises.

For 2000 years Jesus' followers have left their footprints on every part of the earth. Paul began a series of churches and, through his writings and training of young believers, planted the seeds for many others. Not long after Christ commanded the disciples to disseminate his message throughout the world, his followers found their ways into India, Asia, and even China. The Christians who remained in the Holy Land established churches and holy places. All the while, despite the ebb and flow of persecution, each Christian faced the dilemma of choosing a contemplative or active life. Is it better to sit as a monk in a cloister and glorify God in thought, or to be active in the world and glorify God in deed?

In the trial of Jesus we are able to discern the answers to some of the more profound questions of life. A follower of

Jesus is called upon to stand up publicly for the truth, regardless of the cost. The Christian is asked to make a difference, to leave the world a better place with every new generation. The believer is expected to participate in the institutions of the time, meet people where they live, talk to people in terms they can comprehend. The person who understands Jesus' willingness to accept Pilate's decision, and recognizes Pilate's ability to release either Jesus or Barabbas, can see that man does have freedom of choice. We are all constrained by our culture, education, and heritage, but the ultimate responsibility is ours. Pilate allowed Jesus to die. Each person alive today can either accept the eternal life that Jesus offers or ignore it and thereby put it to death.

And choose we must. The choice is not to accept Jesus as some good man, great teacher, or meek-and-mild idealist. Jesus of Nazareth was either the chosen Messiah of the Jews, or he was a fraud, a flim-flam man. There is no middle ground. You must accept him or reject him.

A judge must get to the heart of the issue and not get sidetracked by the details or the clever arguments of counsel. The heart of this matter is as follows:

- Jesus was a real person
- Jesus taught in a real place in time
- Jesus was tried by the Jewish establishment for blasphemy and was found guilty
- Jesus was tried by the Roman establishment for treason and was found not guilty
- Jesus was crucified
- Jesus died and was buried

These facts, I believe, are clear and proven beyond a reasonable doubt. Whether you can take one step further and believe the miracle of his resurrection is something only you

Christ Presented to the People. Etching by Rembrandt, 1655. Unlike most depictions of this scene (see page 155) Rembrandt does not give us a detailed close-up. Rather, he places the viewer away from the crowd at the very back of the courtyard, as if from the perspective of the cowering disciples. Rembrandt's depiction forces us to answer the question: What do you make of Jesus?

can decide. Still, the reliability of the rest of the Gospel is so plain that it is but a small step to believe in the resurrected Christ. And what's more, it would be hard to believe that a man could have such an influence on the world if he had not overcome the ultimate enemy—death.

The teachings of Jesus have changed the world. In 2000 years not a day has gone by when the influence of this itinerant teacher from Nazareth has not been felt. As a trial lawyer, trained to be rational, skeptical, and critical, I believe it improbable that any fraud or false Messiah could have made such a profound impression for good. The most reasonable conclusion, and the most satisfying, is that Jesus was indeed the Son of God, that he was who he claimed to be, and that he did come back to life.

We live in an age of great political show trials, involving issues no less significant than the slavery issue of the 1860s. We live in the midst of moral crises—abortion, pornography, nuclear proliferation, genocide, apartheid, euthanasia, epidemics of suicide, AIDS, violence and international terrorism, and outrageous inequities in material well-being. Daily, these issues are tried in the courts, in the press, in the media, and on the streets. The Christians of the world have many opportunities to participate in these trials, and they know they can offer genuine healing and hope because Jesus, their master, rose from the dead and lives even now. Many, like Peter, will deny that they know Christ. But like infants learning to walk, Christians need to start caring about some issues. This might lead to prayer about those issues. And finally, they may be ready to stand up and take the risk of speaking out in the courtroom of the world—in truth and obedience, like Jesus did so long ago.

The Christian is called to be a light to the world. One man who understood and acted upon his faith was Joseph of Arimathea. The apostle Luke tells us that he, a member of the Sanhedrin, objected to the decisions of that court and asked for Jesus' body. He prepared it lovingly and placed it in his own tomb. What hatred and ridicule he must have faced from his peers. He was the dissenting vote, the traitor to his class, the fool who had faith in the miracle man from Galilee. Luke writes the epitaph for this Joseph of whom we know so little and yet so much: "Joseph, a good and upright man" (Luke 23:50).

In this our age of trials may there be 10,000 men and women like Joseph of Arimathea. Not mythical characters like the Joseph who brought King Arthur's sword to Glastonbury, but real people who take risks for what is right—rational, intelligent Christians, leaders in their communities, willing to be "salt" Christians, acting in faith to give seasoning to a flavorless world. The Holy Spirit is calling those "good and upright" people now. What an honor to be "in" this wonderful world, but "of" the next one.

Now is the time to encourage the faithful to render unto Caesar only that which is Caesar's and to give God all the rest. Give him the best fruits of your time, your labors; give your love to the things that will not tarnish or wither away. The trial of Jesus, and of each one of his followers, goes on every day until he returns. He calls us to be actors in the drama, defenders of the faith, voices of righteousness: "You must be on your guard. You will be handed over to the local councils and flogged in the synagogues. On account of me you will stand before governors and kings as witnesses to them" (Mark 13:9).

But listen. The bailiff has summoned a new jury for the daily retrial of Jesus. Twelve new impartial jurors file into the box and sit down, ready to hear the evidence. Will they believe in Jesus or not?

The judge calls the first witness. What a shock! He has just called out your name.

Appendix

Exhibit A

THE FACTS OF THE TRIAL

A.1 – Complete Composite of the Trial of Jesus Compiled from the Four Gospels

1. Jewish leaders tried to devise a way to destroy Jesus
2. Judas betrayed Jesus
3. Judas led to Jesus those who would arrest him the night of the Passover feast
4. The arrestors were an unidentified crowd sent by the religious leaders—Matthew, Mark
5. The arrestors were temple police—Luke, John
6. The arrestors included a detachment of Roman soldiers—John
7. Judas intended to kiss Jesus at his arrest—Matthew, Mark, Luke
8. Judas kissed Jesus—Matthew, Mark
9. Jesus asked the arrestors whom they sought—John
10. The arrestors replied, "Jesus of Nazareth"—John
11. Jesus replied, "I am he"—John
12. The arrestors fell back on the ground—John
13. Jesus asked the same question again—John
14. The arrestors replied in the same way—John
15. Jesus said, "I told you that I am he; . . . let these men go"—John
16. Someone struck the high priest's servant and cut off his ear—John
17. The servant's name was Malchus—John

183

18. The assailant was a follower of Jesus—Matthew, Luke, John
19. Peter was the assailant—John
20. Jesus told the assailant to cease his resistance—Matthew, Luke, John
21. Jesus healed the high priest's servant's ear—Luke
22. Jesus asked his arrestors if he was being taken as a criminal, and if weapons were necessary. He mentioned that he was available for arrest most every day in the temple, but he was not arrested then—Matthew, Mark, Luke
23. The disciples fled—Matthew, Mark
24. A young man, stripped of his loincloth, fled—Mark
25. Jesus was taken to Annas—John
26. Annas questioned Jesus about his disciples and his teachings—John
27. Jesus refused to answer, and told Annas that he taught openly; therefore, those who heard him should be questioned, not he—John
28. An officer struck Jesus and rebuked him for his reply—John
29. Jesus asked why there were no witnesses and asked why he was struck—John
30. Jesus was taken to the high priest's house that night
31. The high priest and the religious leaders were gathered there—Matthew, Mark
32. Caiaphas was the high priest in question—Matthew
33. Jesus was brought before the religious leaders—Matthew, Mark, Luke
34. The Sanhedrin sought testimony to a charge that was worthy of death, but found none—Matthew, Mark
35. Two false witnesses stated that Jesus had threatened the temple—Matthew, Mark
36. The high priest asked Jesus if he had an answer to the charges against him—Matthew, Mark
37. Jesus remained silent to this question—Matthew, Mark

38. *The Questioning of Jesus before the Sanhedrin*

Jesus was brought before the whole council Friday morning. He was asked if he was the Christ. He responded, "If I tell you, you will not believe me, and if I asked you, you would not answer. But from now on the Son of Man will be seated at the right hand of the mighty God." He was asked if he was the Son of God. Jesus replied, "You are right in saying I am"—Luke

Jesus was brought before the whole council Thursday night. Caiaphas asked if he was the Christ, the Son of God. Jesus replied, "Yes, it is as you say, . . . But I say to all of you: In the future you will see the Son of Man sitting at the right hand of the Mighty One and coming on the clouds of heaven"—Matthew

Jesus was brought before the whole council Thursday night. The high priest asked if he was the Christ, the Son of the Blessed. Jesus replied, "I am, . . . and you will see the Son of Man sitting at the right hand of the Mighty One and coming on the clouds of heaven"—Mark

John makes no mention of an appearance by Jesus before the Sanhedrin.

39. The Sanhedrin was asked if a further witness was necessary, for they had all heard his confession—Matthew, Mark, Luke

40. The high priest asked this of the Sanhedrin—Matthew, Mark

41. The Sanhedrin convicted Jesus and sentenced him to death—Matthew, Mark

42. The decision of the Sanhedrin was unanimous—Mark

43. Jesus was blindfolded—Mark, Luke

44. Jesus was struck repeatedly that night by Jews and was mockingly told to "prophesy" who had hit him—Matthew, Mark, Luke

45. Jesus was verbally abused by the Jews—Luke

46. In the morning, the religious leaders convened to discuss the plan of Jesus' death

47. This assemblage was the Sanhedrin—Mark, Luke

48. Jesus was taken to Pilate

49. Pilate met the Jews outside so that they would not be defiled—John

50. Pilate asked the religious leaders for an accusation against Jesus—John

51. The religious leaders replied that Jesus was a criminal—John

52. Pilate responded that Jesus should therefore be tried according to Jewish law by the Jewish leaders—John

53. The religious leaders replied that they did not have the power to put a man to death—John

54. Jesus was charged by the religious leaders with (a) perverting the nation, (b) forbidding the payment of tribute to Rome, and (c) proclaiming himself king—Luke

55. Pilate asked Jesus, "Are you the king of the Jews?"

56. *The Questioning of Jesus by Pilate*

    Jesus replied to Pilate's question with, "Yes, it is as you say"—Matthew, Mark, Luke

    The discourse of Jesus and Pilate, starting with Jesus' answer to Pilate's question:

    JESUS: "Is that your own idea, . . . or did others talk to you about me?"

    PILATE: "Am I a Jew? . . . It was your people and your chief priests who handed you over to me. What is it you have done?"

    JESUS: "My kingdom is not of this world . . ."

    PILATE: "You are a king, then?"

    JESUS: "You are right in saying I am a king . . . Everyone on the side of truth listens to me."

    PILATE: "What is truth?"—John

57. After the questioning, Pilate told the religious leaders that he found no fault in Jesus—John, Luke

58. Pilate sent Jesus to Herod when he heard that Jesus was a Galilean—Luke

59. Herod questioned Jesus—Luke

60. Jesus remained silent—Luke

61. Herod and his soldiers mocked Jesus—Luke

62. Herod sent Jesus back to Pilate—Luke

63. Pilate told the religious leaders that he had again found no fault in Jesus and neither did Herod—Luke

64. It was a custom that a prisoner was released at the Passover by Pilate—Matthew, Mark, John

65. This release was at the request of the people—Matthew, Mark

66. Jesus was pitted against Barabbas for release

67. Barabbas was a criminal—Matthew, Mark, John

68. Barabbas was a notorious prisoner—Matthew

69. Barabbas committed murder—Mark, Luke

70. Barabbas committed murder during "the insurrection"—Mark

71. The insurrection in which Barabbas was involved was in the city of Jerusalem

72. Claudia warned Pilate to have nothing to do with Jesus—Matthew

73. The religious leaders persuaded the crowd to ask for the release of Barabbas—Matthew, Mark

74. *Barabbas or Jesus?*

    Matthew depicts Pilate asking the crowd whether they want Barabbas or Jesus.

    Mark and John claim Pilate only asked the crowd if they wanted Jesus.

    Luke makes no mention of Pilate even asking the crowd which or whether a prisoner should be released.

75. The crowd cried for Barabbas's release—Matthew, Luke, John

76. Pilate asked the crowd what he should do with Jesus—Matthew, Mark

77. The crowd wanted Jesus crucified—Matthew, Mark, Luke

78. Pilate asked the crowd, "Why? What crime has this man committed?"—Matthew, Mark, Luke

79. Pilate said he found no fault in Jesus—Luke

80. Pilate said he intended to scourge Jesus and release him—Luke

81. The crowd cried more for his crucifixion—Matthew, Mark, Luke

82. Pilate had Jesus scourged—John

83. *The Mocking of Jesus by the Roman Soldiers*

    The Roman soldiers crowned Jesus with a crown of thorns, paid "homage" to him, gave him a sceptre, and otherwise made sport of him.

    Matthew and Mark place the mocking right after the sentencing of Jesus by Pilate.

    Luke makes no reference to a mocking by Roman soldiers.

    John has the mocking taking place at the time of the scourging, before Jesus is sentenced by Pilate.

84. Pilate brought out Jesus to be seen by the crowd—John

85. The crowd cried for Jesus' execution again—John

86. Pilate told the Jews to crucify him themselves—John

87. The religious leaders told Pilate that they had a law by which Jesus should die—John

88. Pilate was frightened when he heard that Jesus claimed to be the Son of God—John

89. Pilate asked about Jesus' origins—John

90. Jesus remained silent—John

91. Pilate reminded Jesus that he had the power of life and death—John

92. Jesus replied that Pilate's power came from above and that Pilate was not as guilty as those who delivered Jesus to him—John

93. Pilate, upon hearing this, sought to release Jesus—John

94. The Jews told Pilate that he would not be a friend of Caesar's if he released Jesus—John

95. At the sixth hour, Pilate presented Jesus to the Jews saying "Here is your king!"—John

96. The crowd once again cried out for Jesus' crucifixion—John

97. Pilate asked if he should crucify their king—John

98. The Jews replied that they have no king but Caesar—John

99. Pilate saw that he was making no progress and that a riot was beginning—Matthew

100. Pilate wished to satisfy the crowd—Mark

101. Pilate said that he was innocent of Jesus' blood, and washed his hands—Matthew

102. Pilate gave sentence for Jesus to be crucified—Luke

103. The mocking of Jesus by the Roman soldiers

104. The soldiers threw dice for Jesus' clothes—John, also see Psalm 22:18

105. Jesus is delivered up to be crucified

106. *Simon the Cyrene Carried the Cross*

    Matthew and Mark make reference to Simon carrying the cross.

    Luke implies that the death march had already begun when Simon was compelled to carry the cross.

107. Jesus was "mourned and wailed" by a crowd that followed him to the place where he was to be crucified—Luke

108. Jesus addressed those who followed him—Luke

109. Jesus was offered wine mixed with gall or myrrh—Matthew, Mark

110. Jesus refused this drink—Matthew, Mark

111. Jesus was crucified between two others

112. The two whom Jesus was crucified with were criminals—Matthew, Mark, Luke

113. Jesus asked forgiveness on those who crucified him—Luke

114. On Jesus' cross was the title "This is the king of the Jews"

115. The religious leaders complained to Pilate that the title on Jesus' cross was wrong; it should state that Jesus "said" he was the king of the Jews—John

116. Pilate refused to change the title—John

117. Passersby mocked Jesus and challenged him to come down off the cross—Matthew, Mark

118. The soldiers who crucified Jesus offered him sour wine and mocked him—Luke

119. Jesus cried out asking God why he had been forsaken—Matthew, Mark

120. The people who gathered around offered him sour wine on a sponge and thought he was calling Elijah to come and rescue him—Matthew, Mark

121. Jesus provided for his mother from the cross—John

122. Jesus said, "Father, into your hands I commit my spirit"—Luke

123. Jesus said, "It is finished"—John

124. Jesus died

125. It was dark from twelve noon to three o'clock in the afternoon—Matthew, Mark, Luke

126. At Jesus' death, there were earthquakes, tombs were opened; some of the dead were raised and seen—Matthew

127. At Jesus' death, the curtain of the temple was torn in two—Matthew, Mark, Luke

128. At Jesus' death the centurion and his men said, "Surely he was the Son of God!"—Matthew, Mark

129. At Jesus' death, the centurion said, "Surely this was a righteous man"—Luke

130. Since Jesus was already dead, he was pierced in the side and blood and water flowed out—John

131. Joseph of Arimathea asked Pilate for the body of Jesus

132. Joseph was a member of the Sanhedrin—Matthew, Luke

133. Joseph was awaiting the kingdom of God—Matthew, Luke

134. Joseph was a disciple of Jesus—Matthew, Luke

135. Joseph's discipleship was kept secret for fear of the Jews—John

136. Joseph was rich—Matthew

137. Joseph had not consented to the Sanhedrin's action against Jesus, for he was a good and righteous man—Luke

138. When Joseph came to Pilate, Pilate was not aware that Jesus had died—Mark

139. Pilate asked a centurion to find out if Jesus was dead—Mark

140. The centurion informed Pilate that Jesus was indeed dead—Mark

141. Pilate gave Joseph leave to take the body—Matthew, Mark, John

142. Joseph wrapped the body in linen and laid it in a tomb cut out of rock

143. Nicodemus helped Joseph—John

144. The tomb was unused—Matthew, Luke, John

145. Joseph rolled the stone against the tomb—Matthew, Mark

146. *Angels at the Tomb*

Matthew and Luke claim there were two angels at the tomb of Jesus.

Mark only describes one angel.

Matthew, Mark, and Luke claim the angel or angels told those present at the tomb that Jesus had risen.

John claims there were two angels, but that Jesus was present in his resurrected form to tell those present that he had risen.

147. *Women at the Tomb*

Matthew and Mark claim Mary Magdalene and Mary, mother of James, were there to see the angel or angels.

Luke claims these two Marys plus Joanna were there to see the angels and the resurrected Jesus.

A.2 – Partial Composite Account:
Details Explicit in One or Two Gospels,
and Consistent with the Other Gospels

1. Judas kissed Jesus—Matthew, Mark

2. The arrestors were representatives (without expressed office) of the religious leaders—Matthew, Mark

3. The arrestors were the temple police—Luke, John

4. The arrestors were a detachment of Roman soldiers—John

5. Jesus asked the arrestors who they sought—John

6. Arrestors replied, "Jesus of Nazareth"—John

7. Jesus replied, "I am he"—John

8. The arrestors fell back on the ground—John

9. Jesus asked the same question again—John

10. Arrestors replied the same way—John

11. Jesus said, "I told you that I am he; . . . let these men go"—John

12. Peter was the assailant of the high priest's servant—John

13. The servant's name was Malchus—John

14. Jesus healed Malchus's ear—Luke

15. The disciples fled—Matthew, Mark

16. Jesus was taken to Annas—John

17. Annas questioned Jesus about his disciples and his teaching—John

18. Jesus would not answer Annas's questions—John

19. An officer struck Jesus and rebuked him for his reply—John

20. Jesus asked why there were no witnesses and why he was struck—John

21. Annas sent Jesus to Caiaphas's house—John

22. The religious leaders were gathered at Caiaphas's house—Matthew, Mark

23. The religious leaders sought testimony to a charge that was worthy of death, but they found none—Matthew, Mark

24. Caiaphas was the high priest who was present—Matthew

25. The high priest asked Jesus if he had an answer to the charges against him—Matthew, Mark

26. Jesus remained silent to this question—Matthew, Mark

27. Upon hearing Jesus' confession, the high priest tore his robes and charged Jesus with blasphemy—Matthew, Mark

28. The high priest asked the council for a decision—Matthew, Mark

29. The council convicted Jesus and sentenced him to death—Matthew, Mark

30. The decision of the council was unanimous—Mark

31. When Jesus was beaten and told to "prophesy" he was blindfolded—Mark, Luke

32. At this time Jesus was also verbally abused—Luke

33. Pilate met the Jews outside so that they would not be defiled—John

34. Pilate asked the religious leaders for an accusation against Jesus—John

35. The religious leaders replied that Jesus was a criminal

36. Pilate responded that Jesus should therefore be tried, convicted, sentenced, and executed according to Jewish law by the Jewish leaders—John

37. The religious leaders replied that they did not have the power to put a man to death—John

38. Jesus was charged by the religious leaders with (a) perverting the nation, (b) forbidding the payment of tribute to Rome, and (c) proclaiming that he was a king—Luke

39. After the questioning, Pilate told the religious leaders that he found no fault in Jesus—John, Luke

40. Pilate sent Jesus to Herod when Pilate heard Jesus was a Galilean—Luke

41. Herod questioned Jesus, mocked him, and sent him back to Pilate—Luke

42. Pilate told the religious leaders again that he found no fault in Jesus and neither did Herod—Luke

43. It was a custom that a prisoner be released by the procurator at the request of the people—Matthew, Mark

44. Barabbas was a notorious prisoner—Matthew

45. Barabbas committed murder—Mark, Luke

46. Barabbas committed murder during "the insurrection"—Mark

47. The insurrection in which Barabbas was involved was in the city—Luke

48. Claudia warned Pilate to have nothing to do with Jesus—Matthew

49. The religious leaders persuaded the crowd to ask for the release of Barabbas—Matthew, Mark

50. Pilate asked the crowd which prisoner they wanted released—Matthew

51. Pilate asked the crowd what he should do with Jesus—Matthew, Mark

52. Pilate said he found no guilt in Jesus—Luke

53. Pilate had Jesus scourged—John

54. Pilate brought out Jesus to be seen by the crowd—John

55. The crowd cried for Jesus' crucifixion again—John

56. Pilate told the Jews to crucify Jesus themselves—John

57. The religious leaders told Pilate that they had a law by which Jesus should die—John

58. Pilate was frightened when he heard that Jesus claimed to be the Son of God—John

59. Pilate asked about Jesus' origins—John

60. Jesus remained silent—John

61. Pilate reminded Jesus that he had the power to release or crucify him—John

62. Jesus replied that Pilate's power came from above, and that Pilate was not as guilty as those who delivered him to Pilate—John

63. Pilate, upon hearing this, sought to release Jesus—John

64. The Jews told Pilate that he would not be Caesar's friend if he released Jesus—John

65. At the sixth hour, Pilate presented Jesus to the Jews saying, "Here is your king"—John

66. The crowd once again cried out for his crucifixion—John

67. Pilate asked if he should crucify their king—John

68. The Jews replied that they had no king but Caesar—John

69. Pilate saw that he was making no progress, and that a riot was beginning—Matthew

70. Pilate wished to satisfy the crowd—Mark

71. Pilate said that he was innocent of Jesus' blood, and washed his hands—Matthew

72. Pilate gave sentence for Jesus to be crucified—Luke

73. Jesus was "mourned and wailed" by a crowd that followed him to the place where he was to be crucified—Luke

74. Jesus addressed those who followed him—Luke

75. Jesus was offered wine mixed with gall or myrrh—Matthew, Mark

76. Jesus refused this drink—Matthew, Mark

77. Jesus asked forgiveness for those who crucified him—Luke

78. Passersby mocked and challenged Jesus to come down off the cross—Matthew, Mark

79. The religious leaders complained to Pilate that the title on Jesus' cross was wrong; it should have stated that Jesus "said" he was king of the Jews—John

80. Pilate refused to change the title—John

81. The soldiers who crucified Jesus offered him sour wine and mocked him—Luke

82. Jesus cried out asking God why he had been forsaken—Matthew, Mark

83. The people who gathered around offered him sour wine on a sponge and thought he was calling Elijah to come and rescue him—Matthew, Mark

84. Jesus said, "Father, into your hands I commit my spirit"—Luke

85. Jesus said, "It is finished"—John

86. At Jesus' death, there were earthquakes, tombs opened, and some of the dead were raised and seen—Matthew

87. At Jesus' death, the centurion and his men said, "Surely, he was the Son of God!"—Matthew, Mark

88. At Jesus' death, the centurion said, "Surely this was a righteous man"—Luke

89. Jesus provided for his mother from the cross—John

90. Since Jesus was already dead, he was pierced in the side and blood and water flowed out—John

91. Joseph of Arimathea was a member of the Sanhedrin who was awaiting the kingdom of God—Matthew, Luke

92. Joseph was a disciple of Jesus—Matthew, Luke

93. Joseph's discipleship was secret for fear of the Jews—John

94. Joseph was rich—Matthew

95. Joseph had not consented to the council's action against Jesus, for he was a good and righteous man—Luke

96. When Joseph came to Pilate, Pilate was not aware that Jesus was already dead—Mark

97. Pilate asked a centurion to find out if Jesus was dead—Mark

98. The centurion informed Pilate that Jesus was indeed dead—Mark

99. Joseph rolled the stone against the tomb—Matthew, Mark

100. Nicodemus helped Joseph with the burial of Jesus—John

A.3 – Composite Account:
Explicit, Consistent Details

1. Jewish leaders tried to devise a way to destroy Jesus
2. Judas betrayed Jesus
3. Judas led those to Jesus who would arrest him
4. Judas intended to kiss Jesus at his arrest (–John)
5. Someone struck the high priest's servant with a sword and cut off his ear
6. The assailant was a follower of Jesus (–Mark)
7. Jesus spoke to the assailant to cease (–Mark)
8. Jesus spoke to his arrestors
9. Jesus asked his arrestors if he was being taken as a criminal, and if weapons were necessary. He mentioned that he was available for arrest most every day in the temple, but he was not arrested (–John)
10. Jesus was taken to a high priest's house (–John)
11. Jesus appeared before the religious leaders (–John)
12. Jesus was questioned by a high priest (–Luke)
13. Jesus was questioned at night (–Luke)
14. Jesus was asked if he was the Christ, or Messiah (–John)
15. Jesus was asked if he was the Son of God, or Son of the Blessed (–John)
16. That night, Jesus kept silent in answer to some questions (–Luke)
17. Jesus was struck repeatedly that night by Jews and was mockingly told to "prophesy" as to who hit him (–John)
18. In the morning, the religious leaders convened to discuss the plan of Jesus' death
19. Jesus was taken to and brought before Pilate
20. Pilate asked Jesus, "Are you the king of the Jews?"
21. Jesus replied, "Yes, it is as you say" (–John)
22. Jesus was pitted against Barabbas for release

23. The crowd cried out for Barabbas's release and Jesus' crucifixion

24. Pilate asked that crowd, "Why? What crime has he committed?" (–John)

25. Jesus was scourged and mocked by the Roman soldiers (–Luke)

26. Pilate delivered Jesus to be crucified

27. Simon the Cyrene carried Jesus' cross to Golgotha (–John)

28. Jesus was crucified between two others

29. These two others were criminals (–John)

30. On Jesus' cross was the title "The King of the Jews" (or something to the same effect)

31. Lots were cast to divide Jesus' clothes

32. The Jewish leaders and one criminal verbally abused Jesus (–John)

33. Jesus was offered sour wine

34. This sour wine was in a sponge which was placed to his lips (–Luke)

35. The sun was darkened from twelve noon to three in the afternoon (–John)

36. Jesus died

37. When Jesus died, the curtain in the temple was torn in two (–John)

38. When Jesus died, the centurion spoke concerning Jesus (–John)

39. Joseph of Arimathea asked Pilate for the body

40. Pilate gave Joseph leave to take the body

41. Joseph wrapped the body in linen and laid it in a tomb cut out of rock

42. The tomb was unused (–Mark)

43. Mary Magdalene went to the tomb early Sunday morning, where she met an angel(s)

44. The angel(s) told Mary that Jesus had risen (–John)

Exhibit B

TIME LINE OF ACCEPTED FACTS

Here is a time line from the year 30 B.C. to A.D. 415, a period of 445 years. Each event listed is a proven fact.

Year	Roman Emperor	Major Events
30 B.C.	Augustus	
23 B.C.		Herod begins construction of the temple
4 B.C.		Death of Herod the Great, division of his kingdom between Herod Archelaus, Herod Philip, and Herod Antipas
4–5 B.C.		Birth of Jesus
A.D. 6		Exile of Archelaus and installation of Coponius as first Procurator of Judea; the "Census Revolt"
14	Tiberius	
26		Pontius Pilate begins his procuratorship
30–33		Death of Jesus
36		Pilate recalled to Rome
37	Gaius Caligula	Herod Agrippa I, King of Judea (until A.D. 44); conversion of Saul at Tarsus
41	Claudius	First Generation of Tannaim
46–48		Apostle Paul's first missionary journey

Year	Roman Emperor	Major Events
50–52		Apostle Paul's second missionary journey
54	Nero	Beginning of Paul's writing activity, and third missionary journey
59–60		Paul taken to Caesarea, then on to Rome
66		Outbreak of the First Jewish Revolt against Rome
68	Galba	Simeon I Patriarch; Second Generation of Tannaim
69	Otho, Vitellius, and Vespasian	
70		Destruction of the temple
73 or 74	Fall of Masada	

MIDDLE ROMAN PERIOD, A.D. 73–180
Writing of the canonical Gospels

Year	Roman Emperor	Major Events
79	Titus	
81	Domitian	
90		Council of Jamnia (Jabneh); Second Generation of Tannaim Apostolic Fathers
96	Nerva	
98	Trajan	
113–117		Jewish Unrest under Trajan
117	Hadrian	Apology of Aristides
125		Babitha writes for more child support
130		Gamaliel II (in Jabneh); Third Generation of Tannaim)
135		Second Jewish Revolt or the Bar Kokhba Revolt: Written records found at Wadi Mu-

Year	Roman Emperor	Major Events
		raba'at; Rabbi Akiba active in Palestine
138	Antonius Pius	
150		Justin Martyr, native of Neapolis in Palestine, debates Trypho in Rome; Diatessaron of Tatian
160		Fourth Generation of Tannaim; Simeon II installed as Patriarch in Galilee
176–192	Commodus (to 192)	

LATE ROMAN PERIOD, A.D. 180–324

Year	Roman Emperor	Major Events
192	Septimus Severus (to 211)	The Apocrypha begins to spread
198		Rabbi Judah the Prince
200	Carcalla (to 217)	
209	Geta (to 212)	Origen (185–254), the Alexandrian Greek scholar, becomes head of Christian theological academy in Caesarea
217	Macrinus	Death of Rabbi Judah the Prince; certification of the Mishnah
218	Elagabalus	
220		Beginnings of the Amoraim; Gamaliel II Patriarch
222	Severus Alexander	
235	Maximinus	
249	Decius	Foundings of synagogues in Palestine; Christian persecutions under Decius; Beginnings of attestation of Christian caves and grottoes

Year	Roman Emperor	Major Events
250		Judah II Patriarch; Second Generation of Amoraim
253	Valerian (to 260) Gallienus (to 268)	
270	Aurelian (to 275)	
276	Probus (to 282)	
280		Gamaliel III Patriarch; Third Generation of Amoraim
284	Diocletian (to 305)	
		Acts of Pilate (Part One)
306	Constantine the Great	
313		Eusebius (260–340) becomes Bishop of Caesarea
320		Judah III and Hillel II Patriarchs; Fourth Generation of Amoraim

BYZANTINE PERIOD, A.D. 324–640

Year	Roman Emperor	Major Events
324		Conversion of Contantine and the "Christianization" of the empire
325		Council of Nicea, first ecumenical council; opening eulogy of Emperor Constantine
333		The Bordeaux Pilgrim visits Palestine
337	Constans (to 350)	Death of Constantine; many synagogues rebuilt and renovated in this general period
351		Revolt of the Jews against Gallus Caesar, 351–53
353	Constantius II	
360		Gamaliel IV and Judah IV Patriarchs; Fifth Generation of Amoraim

Year	Roman Emperor	Major Events
361	Julian (to 363)	Julian's attempt to rebuild the temple
364	Valens I (to 378) Valentinian (to 375)	
379	Theodosius (to 383)	
381		Council of Constantinople; Egeria visits Palestine as Pilgrim
383	Areadius (to 408)	
385		St. Jerome settles at Bethlehem, writes of throngs of religious pilgrims from as far as Persia and Britain
393	Honorius	Acts of Pilate (Part Two)
395		Saint Augustine (354–430) consecrated Bishop of Hippo; Sinaitic Syriac Palimpsest
400		Gamaliel VI is Patriarch; close of Amoraic period
410	Fall of empire	Alaric leads Goths to the destruction of Rome; the Roman Empire had endured 1,163 years
413		Pelagius travels to Palestine
415		Saint Augustine writes *The City of God*

Exhibit C

EXCERPTS FROM THE ACTS OF PILATE

The one Christian apocryphal book that is "on all fours" with the subject of the trial of Jesus is the Gospel of Nicodemus, otherwise known as the Acts of Pilate.

Scholars cannot agree on the complete text of this book, but it is a fascinating example of the painstaking effort of Bible students over the centuries to distinguish reliable historical documents from the fictional, propagandistic manuscripts. With the help of the great scholar Tischendorf, writing in *Evangelia Apocrypha*, we can outline the original source material used to compile the Acts of Pilate:

1. eight early Greek and one early Latin manuscripts
2. three late Greek manuscripts
3. twelve late Latin manuscripts
4. a Coptic papyrus at Turin and some fragments at Paris
5. a Syriac edited by Rahmani in *Studia Syriaca,* II
6. an Armenian edited by Conybeare in *Studia Biblica,* IV (Oxford 1896)

The entire Acts of Pilate is in two parts, the story of the Passion and the Resurrection, first written about A.D. 300 and the Descent into Hell, added sometime after the year A.D. 400. The first part was written to prove that Jesus arose from the dead and that Pilate found him to be innocent of any crime. The second part was written to prove that righteous Jewish fathers were delivered from hell by the atoning death of Christ. The following excerpts are from the first part.

Memorials of Our Lord Jesus Christ
Done in the Time of Pontius Pilate

I, Ananias, the Protector, of praetorian rank, learned in the law,

204

EXHIBIT C   205

did from the divine scriptures recognize our Lord Jesus Christ and
came near to him by faith, and was accounted worthy of holy
baptism: and I sought out the memorials that were made at that
season in the time of our master Jesus Christ, which the Jews
deposited with Pontius Pilate, and found the memorials in Hebrew,
and by the good pleasure of all them that call upon the name of our
Lord Jesus Christ: in the reign of our Lord Flavius Theodosius, in
the seventeenth year, and of Flavius Valentinianus the sixth, in the
ninth indiction [A.D. 425] . . .

In the fifteenth year of the governments of Tiberius Caesar,
Emperor of the Romans, and of Herod, king of Galilee, in the
nineteenth year of his rule, on the eighth of the Kalends of April,
which is the 25th of March, in the consulate of Rufus and Rubellio,
in the fourth year of the two-hundred and second Olympiad, Joseph
who is Caiaphas being high priest of the Jews:

These be the things which after the cross and passion of the Lord,
Nicodemus recorded and delivered unto the high priest and the rest
of the Jews: and the same Nicodemus set them forth in Hebrew
(letters).

I

1. For the chief priests and scribes assembled in council, even
Annas and Caiaphas and Somne and Dothaim and Gamaliel, Judas,
Levi and Nepthalim, Alexander and Jairus and the rest of the Jews,
and came unto Pilate accusing Jesus for many deeds, saying: We
know this man, that he is the son of Joseph the carpenter, begotten
of Mary, and he saith that he is the Son of God and a king;
moreover he doth pollute the sabbaths and he would destroy the
law of our fathers.

Pilate saith: And what things are they that he doeth, and would
destroy the law?

The Jews saith: We have a law that we should not heal any man
on the sabbath: but this man of his evil deeds hath healed the lame
and the bent, the withered and the blind and the paralytic, the dumb
and them that were possessed, on the sabbath day!

Pilate saith unto them: By what evil deeds?

They say unto him: He is a sorcerer, and by Beelzebub the prince
of the devils he casteth out devils, and they are all subject unto him.

Pilate saith unto them: This is not to cast out devils by an unclean spirit, but by the god Asclepius.

2. The Jews say unto Pilate: We beseech thy majesty that he appear before thy judgment-seat and be heard. And Pilate called them unto him and said: Tell me, how can I that am a governor examine a king? They say unto him: We say not that he is a king, but he saith it of himself.

And Pilate called the messenger and said unto him: Let Jesus be brought hither, but with gentleness. And the messenger went forth, and when he perceived Jesus he worshipped him and took the kerchief that was on his hand and spread it upon the earth and saith unto him: Lord, walk hereon and enter in, for the governor calleth thee. And when the Jews saw what the messenger had done, they cried out against Pilate saying: Wherefore didst thou not summon him by an herald to enter in, but by a messenger? for the messenger when he saw him worshipped him and spread out his kerchief upon the ground and hath made him walk upon it like a king! . . .

5. Now when Jesus entered in, and the ensigns were holding the standards, the images [busts] of the standards bowed and did reverence to Jesus. And when the Jews saw the carriage of the standards, how they bowed themselves and did reverence to Jesus, they cried out above measure against the ensigns. But Pilate said unto the Jews: Marvel ye not that the images bowed themselves and did reverence unto Jesus? The Jews say unto Pilate: We saw how the ensigns made them to bow and did reverence to him. And the governor called for the ensigns and saith unto them: Wherefore did ye so? They say unto Pilate: We are Greeks and servers of temples, and how could we do him reverence? for indeed whilst we held the images they bowed of themselves and did reverence unto him.

6. Then saith Pilate unto the rulers of the synagogue and the elders of the people: Choose you out able and strong men and let them hold the standards, and let us see if they bow of themselves. And the elders of the Jews took twelve men strong and able and made them to hold the standards by sixes, and they were set before the judgment-seat of the governor; and Pilate said to the messenger: Take him out of the judgment hall [praetorium] and bring him in again after what manner thou wilt. And Jesus went out of the judgment hall, he and the messenger. And Pilate called unto him

EXHIBIT C   207

them that before held the images, and said unto them: I have sworn by the safety of Caesar that if the standards bow not when Jesus entereth in, I will cut off your head.

And the governor commanded Jesus to enter in the second time. And the messenger did after the former manner and besought Jesus much that he would walk upon his kerchief; and he walked upon it and entered in. And when he had entered, the standards bowed themselves again and did reverence unto Jesus.

II

1. Now when Pilate saw it he was afraid, and sought to rise up from the judgment-seat. And while he yet thought to rise up, his wife sent unto him, saying: Have thou nothing to do with this just man, for I have suffered many things because of him by night. And Pilate called unto him all the Jews, and said unto them: Ye know that my wife feareth God and favoureth rather the customs of the Jews? They say unto him: Yea, we know it. Pilate saith unto them: Lo, my wife hath sent unto me, saying: Have thou nothing to do with this just man: for I have suffered many things because of him by night. But the Jews answered and said unto Pilate: Said we not unto thee that he is a sorcerer? Behold, he hath sent a vision of a dream unto thy wife.

2. And Pilate called Jesus unto him and said to him: What is it that these witness against thee? Speakest thou nothing? But Jesus said: If they had not had power they would have spoken nothing; for every man hath power over his own mouth, to speak good or evil: they shall see to it.

3. The elders of the Jews answered and said unto Jesus: What shall we see? Firstly, that thou wast born of fornication; secondly, that thy birth in Bethlehem was the cause of the slaying of children; thirdly, that thy father Joseph and thy mother Mary fled into Egypt because they had no confidence before the people.

4. Then said certain of them that stood by, devout men of the Jews: We say not that he came of fornication; but we know that Joseph was betrothed unto Mary, and he was not born of fornication. Pilate saith unto those Jews which said that he came of fornication: This you're saying is not true, for there were espousals, as these also say which are of your nation. Annas and Caiaphas say

unto Pilate: The whole multitude of us cry out that he was born of fornication, and we are not believed: but these are proselytes and disciples of his. And Pilate called Annas and Caiaphas unto him and said to them: What be proselytes? They say unto him: They were born children of Greeks, and now are they become Jews. Then said they which said that he was not born of fornication, even Lazarus, Asterius, Antonius, Jacob, Amnes, Zenas, Samuel, Isaac, Phinees, Crispus, Agrippa, and Judas: We were not born proselytes, but we are children of Jews and we speak the truth; for verily we were present at the espousals of Joseph and Mary.

5. And Pilate called unto him those twelve men which said that he was not born of fornication, and saith unto them: I adjure you by the safety of Caesar, are these things true which ye have said, that he was not born of fornication? They say unto Pilate: We have a law that we swear not, because it is sin: but let them swear by the safety of Caesar that it is not as we have said, and we will be guilty of death. Pilate saith to Annas and Caiaphas: Answer ye nothing to these things? Annas and Caiaphas say unto Pilate: These twelve men are believed which say that he was not born of fornication, but the whole multitude of us cry out that he was born of fornication, and is a sorcerer, and saith that he is the Son of God and a king, and we are not believed.

6. And Pilate commanded the whole multitude to go out, saving the twelve men which said that he was not born of fornication, and he commanded Jesus to be set apart: and Pilate saith unto them: For what cause do they desire to put him to death? They say unto Pilate: They have jealousy, because he healeth on the sabbath day. Pilate saith: For a good work do they desire to put him to death? They say unto him: Yea.

III

1. And Pilate was filled with indignation and went forth without the judgment hall and saith unto them: I call the Sun to witness that I find no fault in this man. The Jews answered and said to the governor: If this man were not a malefactor we would not have delivered him unto thee. And Pilate said: Take ye him and judge him according to your law. The Jews said unto Pilate: It is not

EXHIBIT C   209

lawful for us to put any man to death. Pilate said: Hath God forbidden you to slay, and allowed me?

2. And Pilate went in again into the judgment hall and called Jesus apart and said unto him: Art thou the King of the Jews? Jesus answered and said unto Pilate: Sayest thou this thing of thyself, or did others tell it thee of me? Pilate answered Jesus: Am I also a Jew? Thine own nation and the chief priests have delivered thee unto me: what has thou done? Jesus answered: My kingdom is not of this world; for if my kingdom were of this world my servants would have striven that I should not be delivered to the Jews: but now is my kingdom not from hence. Pilate said unto him: Art thou a king, then? Jesus answered him: Thou sayest that I am a king; for this cause was I born and am come, that every one that is of the truth should hear my voice. Pilate saith unto him: What is truth? Jesus saith unto him: Truth is of heaven. Pilate saith: Is there not truth upon earth? Jesus saith unto Pilate: Thou seest how that they which speak the truth are judged of them that have authority upon the earth.

IV

1. And Pilate left Jesus in the judgment hall and went forth to the Jews and said unto them: I find no fault in him. The Jews say unto him: this man said: I am able to destroy this temple and in three days to build it up. Pilate saith: What temple? The Jews say: That which Solomon built in forty and six years, but which this man saith he will destroy and build it in three days. Pilate saith unto them: I am guiltless of the blood of this just man: see ye to it. The Jews say: His blood be upon us and on our children.

2. And Pilate called the elders and the priests and Levites unto him and said to them secretly: Do not so: for there is nothing worthy of death whereof ye have accused him, for your accusation is concerning healing and profaning of the sabbath. The elders and the priests and Levites say: If a man blaspheme against Caesar, is he worthy of death or no? Pilate saith: He is worthy of death. The Jews say unto Pilate: If a man be worthy of death if he blaspheme against Caesar, this man hath blasphemed against God.

3. Then the governor commanded all the Jews to go out from the judgment hall, and he called Jesus to him and saith unto him: What

shall I do with thee? Jesus saith unto Pilate: Do as it hath been given thee. Pilate saith: How hath it been given? Jesus saith: Moses and the prophets did foretell concerning my death and rising again. Now the Jews inquired by stealth and heard, and they say unto Pilate: What needest thou to hear further of this blasphemy? Pilate saith unto the Jews: If this word be of blasphemy, take ye him for his blasphemy, and bring him into your synagogue and judge him according to your law. The Jews say unto Pilate: It is contained in our law, that if a man sin against a man, he is worthy to receive forty stripes save one: but he that blasphemeth against God, that he should be stoned with stoning.

4. Pilate saith unto them: Take ye him and avenge yourselves of him in what manner ye will. The Jews say unto Pilate: We will that he be crucified. Pilate saith: He deserveth not to be crucified.

5. Now as the governor looked round about upon the multitude of the Jews which stood by, he beheld many of the Jews weeping, and said: Not all the multitude desire that he should be put to death. The elder of the Jews said: To this end have the whole multitude of us come hither, that he should be put to death. Pilate saith to the Jews: Wherefore should he die? The Jews said: Because he called himself the Son of God, and a king.

V

1. But a certain man, Nicodemus, a Jew, came and stood before the governor and said: I beseech thee, good lord, bid me speak a few words. Pilate saith: Say on. Nicodemus saith: I said unto the elders and the priests and Levites and unto all the multitude of the Jews in the synagogue: Wherefore contend ye with this man? This man doeth many and wonderful signs, which no man hath done, neither will do: let him alone and contrive not any evil against him: if the signs which he doeth are of God, they will stand, but if they be of men, they will come to nought. For verily Moses, when he was sent of God into Egypt did many signs, which God commanded him to do before Pharaoh, king of Egypt; and there were there certain men, servants of Pharaoh, Jannes and Jambres, and they also did signs not a few, of them which Moses did, and the Egyptians held them as gods, even Jannes and Jambres: and whereas the signs which they did were not of God, they perished

EXHIBIT C   211

and those also that believed on them. And now let this man go, for he is not worthy of death.

2. The Jews say unto Nicodemus: Thou didst become his disciple and thou speakest on his behalf? Did not Caesar appoint him unto this dignity? And the Jews were raging and gnashing their teeth against Nicodemus. Pilate saith unto them: Wherefore gnash ye your teeth against him, whereas ye have heard the truth? The Jews say unto Nicodemus: Mayest thou receive his truth and his portion. Nicodemus saith: Amen, Amen: may I receive it as ye have said.

Notes

Chapter 1—The Gospel Account

1. C. J. Ball, *Apocrypha,* vol. 2 (London: Speakers Comm., 1892), 307.
2. Eusebius, *The History of the Church from Christ to Constantine,* trans. G. A. Williamson (New York: Dorsett, 1984), 53–54.
3. Eusebius, *History of the Church,* 56ff.

Chapter 2—The Historical Setting

1. Pliny, *Fifty Letters of Pliny the Younger* (London: Oxford University Press, 1981), 77.
2. Seneca, *Moral Essays,* trans. John W. Basoe (Cambridge, Mass.: Harvard University Press, 1928), 113.
3. Joseph Derembourg, *Essai sur l'histoire et la géographie de la Palestine* (Paris), 232.
4. Michael Grant, *Jesus: An Historian's Review of the Gospels* (New York: Scribner's Sons, 1977), 200.
5. Tacitus, *The Annals of Tacitus,* ed. H. Furneaux, 2d. ed. (London: Oxford University Press, 1934), 173.
6. Justin Martyr, quoted in Daniel J. Boorstin, *The Discoverers* (New York: Random House, 1983), 15.
7. Maximus of Turin, quoted in Boorstin, *The Discoverers,* 16.

Chapter 3—Modern Archaeology

1. E. M. Blaiklock, *The Archaeology of the New Testament* (Nashville: Nelson, 1984), 12.
2. Yigael Yadin, copy of letter of Babitha, Paris.
3. *Rules of Evidence* (St. Paul, Minn.: West Publishing Co., 1988), Rules 1002–4.

4. Eric M. Meyers and James F. Strange, *Archaeology, the Rabbis, and Early Christianity* (Nashville: Abingdon, 1981), 132.
5. *Rules of Evidence,* Rule 702.
6. Meyers and Strange, *Archaeology,* 125–39.
7. Meyers and Strange, *Archaeology,* 59–60.

Chapter 4—The Reliability of the Gospels

1. *Rules of Evidence,* Rules 803 and 901-B-8.
2. Simon Greenleaf, *A Treatise on the Law of Evidence,* 3 vols. (Salem, N.H.: Ayer, 1972, reprint of 1850 edition), 26.
3. Starkie, *Starkie on Evidence,* quoted in Walter Chandler, *The Trial of Jesus from a Lawyer's Standpoint* (Norcross, Ga.: Harrison, 1976), 7.
4. *Rules of Evidence,* Rules 803–16.

Chapter 5—Ancient Documents

1. C. F. D. Moule, "The Intentions of the Evangelists," *New Testament Essays,* ed. A. J. B. Higgins (Manchester University Press, 1959), 16. See also Edward Gibbon, *The History of the Decline and Fall of the Roman Empire,* I, xvi.
2. E. N. Adler, "Un fragment araméen du Toldot Yeschou," *REJ* 61 (1911), 129.
3. Adler, "Un fragment araméen," 129.
4. Haim H. Ben-Sasson, et al., *History of the Jewish People* (Cambridge, Mass.: Harvard University Press, 1976), 274.
5. J. J. Huldricus, *Historia Jeschuae Nazareni* (Leiden, 1705).
6. Josephus, *Antiquities of the Jews* (Philadelphia: John C. Winston, Standard Edition, n.d.), 535.
7. S. G. F. Brandon, *The Trial of Jesus of Nazareth* (Briarcliff Manor, N.Y.: Stein and Day, 1968).
8. Ian Wilson, *Jesus: The Evidence* (New York: Harper and Row, 1985), 61.
9. Wilson, *Jesus: The Evidence,* 62–64.
10. Tacitus, *Annals,* 168.
11. Pliny, *Fifty Letters,* 43.
12. Joseph L. Davis, in private correspondence with the author, September 10, 1989.

13. Abraham I. Katsch and J. A. Montgomery, *Judaism and the Koran* (New York: A. S. Barnes, 1962), 172.

14. Katsch and Montgomery, *Judaism and the Koran*, quoting Wellhausen.

Chapter 6—The Apocrypha

1. Howard Hanke, *Thompson Chain Reference Bible Survey* (Waco, Tex.: Word, 1981), 1,504.

2. Hennecke and Schneemelcher, "Acts of John," *New Testament Apocrypha*, vol. 2, trans. and ed. R. McL. Wilson (Philadelphia: Westminster Press, 1964), 243.

3. Hennecke and Schneemelcher, "Acts of Pilate," *New Testament Apocrypha*, 444–470.

4. Epistle of Barnabas, see Eusebius, *History of the Church*, 134 and 253.

5. Alfred Lord Tennyson, *Idylls of the King*. Quoting from Sir Thomas Malory's *Morte d'Arthur*, originally published in 1470; Oxford edition by Eugene Vinaver, 1947.

6. A. Zelfelder, "England und das Bazler Konzil," *Historische Studien* (Berlin: Ebering, 1913), 77.

7. Barbara Tuchman, *Bible and Sword* (New York: Ballentine, 1984), 16.

8. William Hone, *The Lost Books of the Bible* (New York: Bell, 1979), 271.

9. Hone, *The Lost Books of the Bible*, 275.

10. Hone, *The Lost Books of the Bible*, 275–76.

11. Guy Schofield, quoted in the introduction to Eusebius, *History of the Church*, 29.

12. Eusebius, *History of the Church*, 66–67.

13. Eusebius, *History of the Church*, 69.

14. Jean Danielou, *The Theology of Jewish Christianity* (Philadelphia: Westminster Press, 1977), 216.

15. Barbara Tuchman, *Bible and Sword*, 27.

Chapter 7—The Hebrew Trial

1. M. LeMann, *Jesus Before the Sanhedrin*, trans. Julius Magath

(Oxford, Ga., 1899). Originally published in Paris as *Valeur de l'assemblée qui prononça la peine de mort contre Jésus Christ.*

2. Maimonides, *Sanhedrin* 17a, 176.

3. Walter Chandler, *The Trial of Jesus,* 29–30.

4. Perkeh Avoth, or "Sentences of the Fathers," iv:8.

5. "Daniel and Susanna," in *The New English Bible with Apocrypha* (London: Oxford University Press, 1970), 204–5.

6. William Barclay, *Bible and History* (Nashville, Abingdon, 1969), 302–3.

Chapter 8—The Roman Trial

1. Josephus, *Antiquities,* 126–27.

2. Josephus, *Antiquities,* 127.

3. Eusebius, *History of the Church,* 80–81.

4. J. I. Packer, *I Want to Be a Christian* (Wheaton, Ill.: Tyndale, 1985), 59.

Chapter 9—The Punishment

1. Richter, quoted in Chandler, *The Trial of Jesus,* 29.

2. William D. Edwards, "On the Physical Death of Jesus Christ," *Journal of the American Medical Association,* 255:11 (April 1986): 1,455–63.

3. Nico Haas, quoted in E. M. Blaiklock, *The Archaeology of the New Testament* (Nashville: Nelson, 1984), 60.

4. Kosegarten, *Chrestomathia Arabica* (1828), 3.

5. Ellis, *History of Madagascar* vol. 1 (London), 371–72.

Chapter 10—The Political Show Trial

1. Aleksandr Solzhenitsyn, *The Gulag Archipelago* (New York: Harper and Row, 1974), 424.

2. Victor Serge, *Memoirs of a Revolutionary* (New York: Writers and Readers, 1974), 330–31.

3. William L. Dwyer, *The Goldmark Case: An American Libel Trial* (Seattle: University of Washington Press, 1984), 246–53.

4. Dwyer, *Goldmark Case,* 246–53.

5. Thomas F. O'Meara, "The Trial of Jesus in an Age of Trials," *Theology Today* (January 1972).

6. C. S. Lewis, *Mere Christianity* (New York: Macmillan, 1978), 56.

Chapter 11—Civil Disobedience

1. S. G. F. Brandon, *The Trial of Jesus of Nazareth* (Briarcliff Manor, N.Y.: Stein and Day, 1968), 141.
2. Brandon, *The Trial of Jesus,* 139.
3. D. R. Catchpole, "The Problem of the Historicity of the Sanhedrin Trial," in *The Trial of Jesus* (Naperville, Ill.: Allenson, 1970), 47–54.
4. Malcolm Muggeridge, *Jesus: The Man Who Lives* (London: Fontana/Collins, 1975), 43.
5. Josephus, *Antiquities,* 535.
6. Edward Gibbon, *The History of the Decline and Fall of the Roman Empire* (Boston: Sampson, 1853), 326.
7. L. Ladurie, *Montaillou—Promised Land of Error* (New York: Random, 1979), 309.
8. Barbara Tuchman, *A Distant Mirror: The Calamitous Fourteenth Century* (New York: Ballentine, 1978), 339.
9. Tuchman, *A Distant Mirror,* 333.
10. Roland Bainton, *The Reformation of the Sixteenth Century* (Boston, Mass.: Beacon, 1952), 20.
11. Albert Schweitzer, *The Quest for the Historical Jesus* (London: E.T. 1910).

Chapter 12—The Closing Argument

1. *Washington Pattern Jury Instructions,* number 2.01. (St. Paul, Minn.: West Publishing Co., 1989), 35–36.
2. C. F. D. Moule, *The Phenomenon of the New Testament* (Manchester: Student Christian Movement, 1967), 63.
3. T. W. Manson, *Studies in the Gospels and Epistles* (Manchester University Press, 1962), 11ff.
4. John Knox, *The Church and the Reality of Christ* (London: Collins, 1963), 42.
5. Michael Grant, *Jesus: A Historian's Review of the Gospels* (New York: Scribner's Sons, 1977), 200.

Bibliography

Adler, E. N. "Un fragment araméen du Toldot Yeschou." *REJ* 61, 1911.

Alfoldi, A. *The Conversion of Constantine and Pagan Rome.* Oxford: E.T., 1948.

Aron, Robert. *Les Années Obscures De Jésus.* Paris: Editions Bernard Grasset, 1960.

Asimov, Isaac. *Guide to the Bible.* New York: Doubleday, 1969.

Bacon, B. W. *Is Mark a Roman Gospel?* Cambridge: Harvard University Press, 1919.

Benny, Philip Berger. *The Criminal Code of the Jews.* London: Smith, Elder and Company, 1880.

Black, M. *An Aramaic Approach to the Gospels and Acts.* Oxford, 1946.

Blaiklock, E. M. *The Archaeology of the New Testament.* Nashville: Thomas Nelson, 1984.

Bonsirven, Joseph. *Testes Rabbiniques des deux premiers siècles chrétiens pour servir a l'intelligence du Nouveau Testament.* Le Vatican, 1957.

Boorstin, Daniel J. *The Discoverers.* New York: Random House, 1983.

Brandon, S. G. F. *The Fall of Jerusalem and the Christian Church.* London, 1951, 2nd ed., 1957, repr. 1968.

_____. "Josephus: Renegade or Patriot?" *History Today,* vol. VIII, 1958.

_____. "The Date of the Markan Gospel" *N.T.S.,* vol. VII, 1960–61.

_____. *Man and His Destiny in the Great Religions.* Manchester University Press, 1962.

_____. "Herod the Great." *History Today,* vol. XII, 1962.

_____. *History, Time and Deity,* Manchester University Press, 1965.

_____. "Matthaean Christianity." *The Modern Churchman,* vol. VIII, 1965.

_____. *Jesus and the Zealots.* Manchester University Press, 1967.

Bruce, F. F. *The Acts of the Apostles.* London, 1951.

_____. "Christianity under Claudius." *B.J.R.L.,* vol. 44, 1962.

Bultmann, R. "History and Eschatology in the New Testament." *N.T.S.,* vol. I, 1954–55.

_____. *The Theology of the New Testament.* E.T., vol. I, London, 1959.

Carrington, P. *The Early Christian Church.* 2 vols. Cambridge, 1957.

Catchpole, D. R. *The Trial of Jesus.* Naperville, Ill.: Allenson, Inc., 1970.

Chandler, Walter M. *The Trial of Jesus from a Lawyer's Standpoint.* Norcross, Ga.: Harrison, 1925, 1976.

Clarke, W. K. L. *New Testament Problems.* London, 1929.

Cullmann, Oscar. *The State in the New Testament,* New York: Scribner's, 1956.

Daniel, C. "Esseniens, zélotes et sicaires et leur mention par paranymie dans le N.T." *Numen,* XIII, 1966, Leiden.

Daniel, Rops. *Histoire Sainte: Le peuple de la Bible.* Paris: Fayard, 1943.

Danielou, Jean. *The Theology of Jewish Christianity.* Philadelphia: Westminster Press, 1977.

Daube, D. *The New Testament and Rabbinic Judaism.* London, 1956.

Derembourg, Joseph. *Essai sur l'histoire et la géographie de la Palestine (d'après les Thalmuds et autres sources rabbiniques).* Paris, 1867.

Deutsch, Emanuel. *The Talmud*. Philadelphia: The Jewish Publication Society of America, 1896.

Dodd, C. H. "The Fall of Jerusalem and the 'Abomination of Desolation.'" *J.R.S.*, vol XXXVII, 1953–54.

_____. *Historical Tradition in the New Testament*, Cambridge, 1963.

Doyle, A. D. "Pilate's Career and the Date of the Crucifixion." *J.T.S.*, vol. XLII, 1941.

Edersheim, Alfred. *The Life and Times of Jesus the Messiah*. New York: Longmans, Green and Company, 1905.

Eisler, R. *The Messiah Jesus and John the Baptist*. English edition. London: A.H. Krappe, 1931.

Ernest, Joseph. *Histoire des origines due christianisme*. Paris: Renan, 1863.

Eusebius, *The History of the Church from Christ to Constantine*. New York: Dorsett, 1965.

Farrar, Frederic W. *The Life of Christ*. New York: E. P. Dutton and Company, 1883.

Fisher, George Park. *The Beginnings of Christianity*. New York: Charles Scribner's Sons, 1906.

_____. *Manual of Christian Evidences*. New York: Charles Scribner's Sons, 1900.

Gibbon, Edward. *The History of the Decline and Fall of the Roman Empire*. Boston: Sampson, 1853.

Goguel, Maurice. *La Naissance du Christianisme*. Paris: Payot, 1946.

Gough, M. *The Early Christians*. London, 1961.

Graetz, H. *Sinai et Golgotha, ou les Origines du Judaisme et du Christianisme*. Paris: Michel Levy, 1867.

Grant, F. C. *The Economic Background of the Gospels*. Oxford, 1926.

Grant, Michael. *Jesus: A Historian's Review of the Gospels*. New York: Charles Scribner's Sons, 1977.

Greenidge, A. H. J. *The Legal Procedure of Cicero's Time*. London: Stevens & Sons, 1901.

Guignebert, Charles. *Le monde juif vers le temps de Jésus.* Paris, 1935.

Hennecke, E., and Schneemelcher, W. (eds.). *New Testament Apocrypha,* R. McL. Wilson, vol. I. Philadelphia: Westminster Press, 1964.

Hone, William. *The Lost Books of the Bible.* New York: Bell, 1979. (Reprint of 1926 World Pub. Co. edition.)

Hort, F. J. *Judaistic Christianity.* London, 1894.

Huldricus, J. J. *Historia Jeschuae Nazareni.* Leiden, 1705.

Innes, A. Taylor. *The Trial of Jesus Christ.* Edinburgh: T. and T. Clark, 1905.

James, M. R. *The Apocryphal New Testament.* Oxford, 1926.

Jeremias, J. *Jerusalem zur Zeit Jesu.* I, II. Teil, 2. Aufl. Gottingen, 1958

Josephus. *Antiquities of the Jews.* Philadelphia: John C. Winston, Standard Edition, n.d.

Jost, I. M. *The Works of Flavius Josephus.* Leipzig: Dorffling und Francke, 1857.

Katsch, Abraham I., and Montgomery, J.A. *Judaism and the Koran.* New York: A. S. Barnes, 1962.

Kraeling, C. H. "The Episode of the Roman Standards at Jerusalem." *H.Th.R.,* vol. XXXV, 1942.

de Labriolle, P. *La réaction päienne: étude sur la polemique antichrétienne du Ier au Vme siècles.* Paris, 1942 (1934).

Ladurie, LeRoy. *Carnival in Romans.* New York: George Braziller, Inc., 1979.

_____. *Montaillou—Promised Land of Error.* New York: Random House, 1979.

Latourette, Kenneth Scott. *A History of Christianity.* New York: Harper and Brothers, 1953.

Lerclercq, H. *La vie chrétienne primitive.* Paris, 1928.

Lewis, C. S. *God in the Dock.* Grand Rapids: Eerdmans, 1970.

Lippman, Thomas W. *Understanding Islam.* New York: New American Library, 1982

Loewe, H. *"Render unto Caesar": Religious and Political Liberty in Palestine.* Cambridge, 1940.

Mendelsohn, S. *The Criminal Jurisprudence of the Ancient Hebrews.* Baltimore: M. Curlander, 1891.

Meyers, Eric M., and Strange, James F. *Archaeology, the Rabbis, and Early Christianity.* Nashville: Abingdon, 1981.

The Mishnah. Trans. H. Danby. Oxford, 1933.

Moffatt, J. *An Introduction to the Literature of the New Testament.* 3rd rev. ed. Edinburgh, 1933.

Moule, C. F. D. "The Intentions of the Evangelists." In *New Testament Essays.* Manchester, 1959.

Muggeridge, Malcolm. *Jesus: The Man Who Lives.* London: Fontana/Collins, 1975.

Nantet, Jacques. *Les Juifs et les Nations.* Paris: Editions du Minuit, 1956.

Neutestamentliche Apokryphen. Hrg. E. Hennecke, and W. Schneemelcher. Tubingen: I. Band, 1959.

Packer, J. I. *I Want to Be a Christian.* Wheaton, Ill.: Tyndale, 1985.

Perowne, Stewart. *Hérode le Grand et son époque.* Trans. Nathalie Gara. Paris: Hachette, 1958.

Pfeiffer, Charles F. *The Dead Sea Scrolls and the Bible.* New York: Weathervane Books, 1969.

Rapa, Jonah. *Pilpul al zeman zemanim zemannehem.* London, 1908.

Robinson, Maxine. *Muhammad.* New York: Pantheon, 1980.

Roth, C. *Historical Background of the Dead Sea Scrolls.* Oxford: Blackwell, 1958.

Salvador, J. *Jésus-Christ et sa doctrine, histoire de la naisance de l'Eglise, de son organisation et de ses progrès pendant le I siècle.* Paris: Guyot et Scribe, 1838.

Schweitzer, Albert. *The Quest for the Historical Jesus.* London: E.T., 1910.

Simon, M. *Verus Israel: étude sur les rélations entre Chrétiens et Juifs dans l'Empire Romain (135–425).* Paris, 1948.

Solzhenitsyn, Aleksandr I. *The Gulag Archipelago*. New York: Harper and Row, 1974.

Stauffer, E. *Christus und die Caesaren*. Hamburg, 1952.

Stone, I. F. *The Trial of Socrates*. New York: Doubleday, 1988.

Stott, John R. W. *The Cross of Christ*. Downers Grove, Ill.: InterVarsity, 1986.

Strack, H. L., and Billerbeck, P. *Kommentar zum Neuen Testament aus Talmud und Midrasch*. Munich: 4 Bande, 1922–28.

Suetonius. *Lives of the Caesars*. Ed. C. L. Roth. Leipzig, 1891.

Tacitus, *Annales, Historiae*. Ed. C. Halm. 2 vols. Leipzig, 1891.

_____. *The Annals of Tacitus*. Ed. H. Furneaux. 2nd ed. Oxford, 1934.

Toynbee, Arnold, ed. *The Crucible of Christianity*. New York: World Publishing, 1969.

Tuchman, Barbara. *Bible and Sword*. New York: Ballentine, 1984.

_____. *A Distant Mirror: The Calamitous Fourteenth Century*. New York: Ballentine, 1978.

Wilson, Edmund. *Israel and the Dead Sea Scrolls*. New York: Farrar, Straus, Giroux, 1954, 1978.

Winter, P. *On the Trial of Jesus*. Berlin, 1961.

Yadin, Y. *The Scroll of the War of the Sons of Light against the Sons of Darkness*. Oxford, 1962.

_____. "The Excavation of Masada, 1963/64. Preliminary Report." *Israel Exploration Journal*. Jerusalem, vol. XV (1965). Masada, E.T., London, 1966.

Zahrnt, H. *The Historical Jesus*. London: E.T., 1963.

Zeitlin, S. *Who Crucified Jesus?* New York, 1942.

Zelfelder, A. "England un das Bazler Konzil." *Historische Studien*. Berlin: Ebering, 1913.